D1156669

LIES, DAMNED LIES

AND SOME EXCLUSIVES

Henry Porter

CHATTO & WINDUS

THE HOGARTH PRESS
London

UNIVERSITY
OF NEW BRUNSWICK

MAY 7 198

LIBRARIES

Published in 1984 by
Chatto & Windus · The Hogarth Press
40 William IV Street
London WC2N 4DF

All rights reserved. No part of this publication
may be reproduced, stored in a retrieval system, or
transmitted in any form, or by any means,
electronic, mechanical, photocopying or otherwise,
without the prior permission of the publisher.

British Library
Cataloguing in Publication Data

Porter, Henry
Lies, damned lies and some exclusives.
1. Fraud in newspaper reporting – Great Britain
– History – 20th century
I. Title
070.4'3'0941   PN5124.F7

ISBN 0 7011 2841 0

Copyright © Henry Porter 1984

Phototypeset by Wyvern Typesetting Limited, Bristol
Printed in Great Britain by
Redwood Burn Ltd
Trowbridge
Wiltshire

CONTENTS

ACKNOWLEDGMENTS

I would first like to thank Angela Pitts, the *Daily Mirror* journalist who carried out exhaustive and highly efficient research for this book. Sadly I cannot be so specific in my gratitude to the other Fleet Street journalists who gave me help and encouragement but who cannot for obvious reasons be mentioned by name here. I am similarly restrained in thanking the press officers of countless organisations who do not want to sever entirely their relations with the national press, however tempting that may be. Among those I *can* thank are Mary Brooke, whose conversation led me to the idea for *Lies, Damned Lies* . . .; Jane Clarke and Karen Sharpe, who typed my often illegible manuscript at great speed; Mike Petty, the very patient editor; and finally the Worm who gave me the title.

In memory of the artist
MICHAEL HARRISON

You cannot hope to bribe or twist
(Thank God) the British Journalist.
Considering what the chap will do
Unbribed, there's no occasion to.
HUMBERT WOLFE

CHAPTER 1

The Paper You Can Trust

An observant reader of the *Daily Telegraph* might have noticed the remarkable frequency with which one Raphael Dunvant cropped up in the paper's news pages. At one stage during the late seventies little of a newsworthy nature seemed to happen without his colourful participation. From Dunvant's many appearances we gather that he came from a military background, owned a modest estate in Gloucestershire, was fiercely patriotic and was constantly bemoaning the decline in standards of morality and service in British life. The paper's first encounter with Dunvant came on the eve of the Queen's Silver Jubilee celebrations, when he was found in a large crowd outside Buckingham Palace waiting for the procession on the following day. Then he limited himself to the view that the state ought to supply the crowd with large brown paper bags in which to spend the night; since there were none he was proposing to jam his shooting-stick into a crack in the pavement and sit in rigid vigil for his monarch.

Thereafter he began to appear with increasing regularity. On one occasion he launched a furious attack on the designs of Tony Benn and the Labour Party on the acres of the landed gentry. On another he complained of the slack service of salesgirls in Fortnum and Mason; a sharp slap on the bottom improved their speed and efficiency, he advised. A few months later he was found, sitting under a palm tree four hundred and fifty miles up the Congo, by the equally improbable figure of Brigadier Blashford-Snell. At the time the paper reported that there were fears for this strange Englishman's health, but he seems to have recovered sufficiently to molest a party of boy scouts on a camping trip to Scotland. There was no end to his exploits, and it seemed as if the paper need only to follow Dunvant on his peregrinations to fill its columns with entertaining stories conveniently encapsulating all the quirkiness and conservatism of the average *Daily Telegraph* reader.

It was all too good to be true. This, in fact, was precisely the case. Dunvant was entirely the creation of a fertile mind in the *Telegraph* newsroom. His creator's secret, which over the months was shared with most of the reporting staff, was to cast Dunvant in a dazzling cameo part rather than in the leading role of any particular story, to perform engagingly for a few paragraphs as a witness to, or victim of, some large event. However, sometimes the quality of his performance was such that the *Telegraph* sub-editors promoted him from the middle of a story to the top. His creator came dangerously near exposure when, in a fairly routine weather story, he reported that Dunvant's leg-iron had been struck by lightning while he umpired a cricket-match in north-east England. Naturally the journalists of north-east England were annoyed that they had missed such a splendid local story, particularly as it appeared as the second lead on the front of a national newspaper. They rang the *Telegraph* with a view to finding the survivor, interviewing him and photographing the smouldering and deformed leg-iron. Oddly, nobody at the *Telegraph* could help, and an exhaustive check of the local hospitals in the Newcastle area produced nothing.

Dunvant's glorious career came to an end after a largely fictitious report about football hooliganism. He was travelling by train to Scotland with his friend, Mr Pagett-Soames, this time in pursuit of salmon rather than boy scouts. The pair were set upon by fans celebrating their international victory over England, and Dunvant's prized salmon rods were snapped over his head. The report duly went into the paper, and all would have been well had not the Scots editor of the *Sunday Express*, Sir John Junor, who prides himself on an instinct for the bogus, wondered why these two gentlemen were going salmon-fishing when salmon were out of season. He voiced his suspicions to one or two senior executives of the *Telegraph*, who were unable to supply an explanation. The culprit took fright and immediately decided to kill

Dunvant off, but before doing so he had to exhume him from the cuttings library and excise his many references. It proved an impossible job, and I am told that, such is the excellence of the paper's cuttings service, the odd mention of Dunvant may occasionally be found in some obscure file on Cricket Umpiring or Expeditions: West Africa.

The success of Dunvant shows how easy it is to insert outlandish fiction in an apparently straightforward news report. Nobody, let alone the seasoned staff of the *Daily Telegraph* (which advertises itself as The Paper You Can Trust) thought to question Dunvant's existence or his extraordinary antics. In fact it seems that Dunvant had a number of fictitious friends, aside from Pagett-Soames; Mr Henry Cincinnati, for example, who corresponded at length with the letters page on the pressing issue of traffic congestion on Malta.

The private enjoyment to be had from this faking is matched by the risk the perpetrators run. Still, it proves irresistible to some of us entrusted with recording the world and its bewildering variety of events each day. I should confess here to telling a friend on what was then the *Evening Standard* that I had just seen a black cat killed outright by a hailstone. He wrote a small italic paragraph about the incident and six months later the *Daily Telegraph*, in the shape of Guy Rais, unwittingly included my fake cat in his review of the year's weather.

H.L. Mencken, the great American journalist, admits in his essay *The Synthesis of News* that, having been introduced to the art of fiction by a reporter named De Bekker, he found it hugely enjoyable and useful too. 'If under his inspiration,' he says, 'we reported that a mad dog had run amok and bitten twenty children, there was always an actual dog in the background and our count of the victims would be at least as authentic as any cops would make it.' Such reports gained credibility in the eyes of his editor because the accounts in rival newspapers agreed with him on such basic details as names, ages and addresses. It is still true today that Fleet Street editors and their staff seek confirmation of their own paper's accuracy by looking at their rivals.

Mencken recalls that his faking enjoyed a dangerous recrudescence when he became managing editor (two or three positions down from the Editor) on the *Baltimore Evening Herald*: 'My masterpiece of all time was a synthetic dispatch printed in 1905.' To cut a tall story short, Mencken and his news editor decided that theirs would be the first paper to carry a detailed account of the great naval battle between Russia and Japan. Everyone knew that the two fleets had engaged but only the vaguest rumours had reached America. Mencken and his collaborator read all they could find on the subject and then put together an authoritative piece dwelling on the strengths and weaknesses of each fleet, their different tactics and the names and numbers of ships lost. With incredible nerve he declared that the day was Japan's. The story stole two weeks on the opposition and to Mencken's eternal delight he was proved accurate in all but the smallest detail; his account was even confirmed by a Japanese naval historian writing thirty years later.

It would be ludicrous to censure Mencken now, if only because his fictional reports were of such a very high standard. However, it should be said that there was method in his mischief. The practice of making up entire tracts of his paper saved him considerable time and effort, often produced a more sensational and thus more readable story than his rivals, and certainly helped satisfy his paper's daily demands for copy. These factors still preoccupy the minds of journalists today. Although the space available is, perhaps, less, the competition is at least as tough and reporters, never the most diligent profession, are just as eager to use the occasional labour-saving device.

It is the contention of this book that fiction of all sorts appears in nearly every section of the national press. Some of the examples from 1983 are as entertaining as the Dunvant hoax, but there are others where it is difficult to raise much of a laugh. This is because when a newspaper lies it exploits its readership in two ways. The first and most obvious is that the reader may fairly expect to get an accurate version of events when he buys a newspaper; if, in reality, he is getting a frothy concoction of falsehood, inaccuracy and downright dishonesty, he is being cheated. Second, it is frequently the case, as in the story that follows, that the public themselves are the victims of newspaper lies.

Three years ago it came out that a woman had hidden her husband from the police for eight years. He had, it seems, absconded from the army and spent most of the time under the floorboards of their home.

The northern news desks of the popular nationals perceived that there was an interesting interview to be had from his wife and dispatched their reporters with instructions to get as much out of her as possible. The only obstacle to their plans was that the woman was almost totally monosyllabic. One reporter, from the *Daily Star*, encouraged her to say a little but it was rather too bland for the projection his and the other papers had in mind. The rest got nowhere, so they agreed that, using such quotes as the *Daily Star* had managed to winkle out of her, they would compose an interview containing all the observations that a woman who had lived with a secret might make. The results were lively, and were well-used the next day. The news editors were presumably satisfied, while their reporters were safe in the knowledge that their combined testament would outweigh any objections the woman might raise; it was clear to them in any case that she had not the wit to protest in even the most superficial way.

Talking to one of the reporters afterwards, I learnt that none of them had the slightest qualm. She argued that all they had done was to lend a certain eloquence to the woman's story and that her reputation would consequently have been enhanced. Moreover, if she turned in a piece based on the quotes as uttered she would have been told to rewrite it and add what is known as 'top-spin'. This was a new euphemism to me; it refers to the artificial additive and colouring newspapers employ to make a story appetising. Perhaps, as she argued, such flavouring does no harm. The consumer has been entertained and anyway the story of the woman and her husband is very soon forgotten. Mr Rupert Murdoch put the same view more succinctly when the Hitler Diaries were finally revealed to be the work of a cheap conman: 'After all,' he said, 'we are in the entertainment business.' By this definition every sly invention, exaggeration and embellishment is justified.

This low regard for the truth spreads elsewhere in newspapers. What chance, for instance, is there of reporters taking care over facts if in another part of their publication colleagues are actively encouraged to develop the creative ability of a novelist? Similarly, it takes no great leap of imagination to see that the scruples involved in reporting events and issues that determine the way we are governed will be few. And then, of course, there are the stories which newspapers, for one reason or another, would prefer to leave uncovered. A recent case of this interested negligence was the reluctance of Fleet Street's financial journalists to write about the breach of trust aspects of the newspaper proprietors' sale of the Reuters international news agency. Truth, therefore, is as easily compromised by omission as by commission.

I have no special qualification or taste for sermonising, but it does seem to me that if a large section of the media continues to distort, dissemble and omit, we may as well resign ourselves to some dismal tyranny where these practices are the norm. It can be argued that the credibility of the press, and that is surely what is at stake, is pretty well intact. Newspapers continue to be sold in huge numbers and there is no real evidence that the readers persistently mistrust what is written in them, even if journalists are regularly placed alongside tax collectors and used-car dealers in surveys of public esteem. My own view is that this continuing trust in the content of newspapers is due to a wholly understandable ignorance on the consumer's part. Were he to be made conscious of the level of fiction and inaccuracy in the press, he might just begin to lose faith and, one hopes, to demand a better service.

This, then, is the reason for assembling examples of less than accurate journalism from 1983. It is by no means a complete survey of a year in which Fleet Street newspapers, from the most self-regarding to the seediest, excelled themselves in their lack of concern for such simple matters as truth.

CHAPTER 2

Tales of Mystery
and Imagination

It is a telling fact of newspaper life that journalists, especially in the popular end of the business, prefer to use the words 'story', 'tale', and even 'yarn'. Such terms imply a fictional narrative and, indeed, are still largely understood to do so by those outside the newspaper industry. 'Report' or 'account', on the other hand, suggest a straightforward record of facts or events. Perhaps this choice of words reveals a subconscious admission that newspaper stories often contain a strong fictional element. Certainly other phrases from newspaper argot confirm the suspicion that accuracy is not the highest priority among journalists. If, for instance, I were to congratulate a fellow scribe on a recent article I would say, 'That was a good read,' or 'You got a decent show with that piece,' thus emphasising entertainment value and prominence rather than accuracy. Then there is the phrase, 'sexy story', which has nothing to do with sex but refers to a piece so sensational as to give approximately the same satisfaction, at least to the journalist. One of the highest compliments you can pay a journalist is to call him a 'good operator'. This covers a multitude of shady practices but generally describes a reporter who is good at getting to the subject of a news story and if necessary shielding the subject from the attentions of his rivals. He has, in the words of Nicholas Tomalin, a 'rat-like cunning', is fast but judicious with the newspaper's chequebook, makes the most of his material and files his copy on time. There is little interest in the accuracy of a good operator's stories, merely in his ability to get away with elastic treatment of facts and quotes. The most interesting phrase I

have yet encountered in newspaper offices was used by a Scottish gossip
columnist who urged subordinates who failed to stand a story up to
'shepherd the facts, laddie, shepherd the facts'; which taken in its most
literal sense means to corral a number of unrelated facts into a story and
produce an effect which in all probability has no bearing either on what
has happened or on what will happen, but is nonetheless a thoroughly
good 'read'.

It would be a mistake to read any huge significance into the jargon of
newspaper offices; still, I offer it as a small indication that sensation is
generally the journalist's overriding concern, and one which is
detrimental to the interests of the truth. Over the last decade or so this
addiction to sensationalism has grown to the point where some
newspaper reporters have begun to resemble the compulsive liars
occasionally to be found among schoolchildren; they frequently confuse reality with fiction, their fantasies are so outrageous as to be
immediately detectable and even after exposure they return to the habit.
Consider the case of Mrs Marica McKay, the widow of Sergeant Ian
McKay, who was posthumously awarded one of two Victoria Crosses of
the Falklands campaign. When the awards were announced two
newspapers, the *Daily Mirror* and the *Sun*, carried interviews with the
widows of the dead soldiers. The *Mirror* presented the article as an
'Exclusive' while the *Sun* went the whole way and announced grandio-
sely that it had a 'World Exclusive'. That was the paper's first lie. Under
the headline THE PRIDE AND HEARTBREAK OF TWO VCS'
WIDOWS the story began:

> VC's widow Marica McKay fought back her tears last night and
> said: 'I'm so proud of Ian, his name will remain a legend in the
> history books forever.' . . . Hugging her children at their home in
> Rotherham, Yorkshire, she said: 'I'm proud of Ian's Victoria
> Cross . . . but I'd exchange all the medals in the world to have him
> back.'

It is a very good test of newspaper accuracy to read quotes like these
aloud and ask yourself whether they are the sort of thing someone might
really say. Would the response of a grieving widow have been 'his name
will remain in the history books forever'? The answer is, of course, no.

The only explanation is that John Kay, the journalist under whose name the interview appeared, inserted this touchingly brave sentiment himself. This was more or less the case although the Press Council's investigation of the matter established that Kay did not even dream up the quotes himself. This was left to some obliging secretaries at the *Sun*'s offices in Bouverie Street. He just put them in at the right place.

The *Sun*, then, was found guilty of an obvious fraud, outrageous and easy to detect, yet John Kay and the editor, Kelvin Mackenzie (who as Kay told the Press Council was fully aware of his fabrication), nearly escaped without criticism. Kay's most stupid mistake was to date the story by the phrase 'fought back the tears last night'. For on the night in question Mrs McKay was not in her home at Rotherham but in the Howard Hotel in London talking to representatives of the *Daily Mirror*. Not a little jealous of its own exclusive, the *Mirror* made some investigations and concluded that the *Sun*'s World Exclusive was nothing but a cheap fabrication. In a famous leader entitled 'Lies, Damned Lies and *Sun* Exclusives' the *Mirror* castigated Mackenzie and the *Sun* for its behaviour – and, incidentally, provided this book with its title. What is perhaps most extraordinary about the whole affair is that it was only due to the mischievousness of Peter Hillmore, the *Observer*'s diarist, who encouraged his secretary Caroline Metcalfe to complain to the Press Council, that the matter was put before it. In the event it was not until August 1983 that the Council addressed itself to this 'deplorable, insensitive deception of the public'. It was then that the *Sun*, in the shape of Kenneth Donlan, a former editor of the *News of the World*, displayed a very loose grasp on reality and everyday ethics. Instead of admitting and regretting the falsehood, Donlan attempted to mitigate his newspaper's action by complaining that the *Sun*'s journalists had not been able to talk to Mrs McKay because she was with the *Daily Mirror*. He said the staff were under strict instructions not to allow any harassment of the widow and went on to describe an unpleasant scene at the Howard Hotel. Sadly it did not occur to anyone at the Press Council to point out that the unpleasant scene was almost certainly caused by the appearance of the *Sun* reporters, and moreover that Donlan was advancing the presence of the *Daily Mirror* as an argument for making up an interview. Throughout the hearing Donlan maintained that the quotes used in Kay's piece were drawn from other newspapers, principally the *Daily Express* and the *Daily Mirror*, and an unscreened ITN interview with Mrs McKay's mother. Even if this was so – the Press Council did not accept it – the paper was still guilty of gross dishonesty in giving the impression that it talked to Mrs McKay in person, and of course in the use of the 'World Exclusive' tag. After reading the Council's adjudication one is left with the impression of an unattractive little boy who has been caught lying and refuses to admit it.

Earlier in the year Donlan had appeared before the Council in roughly similar circumstances, although in this case the *Sun* was guilty of an even more ludicrous fabrication. It seems that a reporter named George Forbes had been sent along to cover the shooting of a Monty Python film, which included the usual cast of John Cleese, Michael Palin and Terry Jones. The intention of the director was to include a scene of the Battle of Rorke's Drift, and to achieve a certain verisimilitude he hired 120 coloured extras through the community relations office. They were asked to dress up in Zulu costumes and act in a warlike manner in front of the cameras. However, for reasons that were never entirely clear, the ersatz Zulus went on strike and refused to stage the battle. Mr Forbes reported this as follows:

> After the black warriors downed spears, the heavens opened and long-legged Cleese leaped about among the extras shouting, 'Which of you bastards did a rain dance?'

This was just the sort of incident that Forbes had been sent to pick up and it was precisely the sort of joke which appealed to executives at the *Sun*. The only problem was that John Cleese denied saying anything of the sort. He complained to the *Sun*'s editor, offering Mr Mackenzie £10,000 if he could prove that he actually behaved in the way reported. Mackenzie failed to provide corroboration so Cleese took the matter to the Press Council, where Mr Forbes adopted a concern for the exploitation which, in view of the *Sun*'s stance on racial matters, was pure humbug: 'He should think himself lucky that it was a humorous article as the film unit was using semi-naked black labour at a pittance to dress up in outfits . . . and die in front of British guns.'

Perhaps it was at this point that the Council's Complaints Committee became convinced that Cleese had said no such thing. After their adjudication was published, Forbes still maintained his innocence, however.

It is a temptation in this book, particularly in a chapter devoted to the senseless fantasies of newspaper reporters, to concentrate on the output of the *Sun*. Other newspapers are just as guilty, even if less obviously so.

The *Daily Express*, now under the control of Larry Lamb, who was knighted after more than a decade of service at the *Sun*, persistently proves the rule that the word 'Exclusive' is immediate grounds for suspicion. The news in the 'fact-packed *Daily Express*' of November 17, 1983, was that President Andropov had been shot. The headline read WAS ANDROPOV SHOT?, which every sub-editor know means ANDROPOV WAS SHOT. The writer, David Kyle, reported that the disappearance of the Soviet leader from public view could be explained by the fact that he had recently had a row with the late Leonid Brezhnev's son, Yuri, who had pulled a gun and wounded him in the arm. Unrestrained by fears of an official denial or a Press Council hearing, Mr Kyle warmed to his theme, painting a picture of family feuds, violence and intrigue – a sort of Soviet version of *Dynasty*. Here is his description of Brezhnev junior:

> He is known to western intelligence men to be a hot-tempered man who enjoys the high-life and who is, like his father, an expert with a gun. The Brezhnev family had for some years secretly leased a hunting estate in Tanzania.

There then followed a long and baffling account of how the families had done each other down, the purpose of which was to prove that Brezhnev's only course of action was to bowl along to the Kremlin and take a pot at Andropov.

One wonders how seriously the *Daily Express* took Mr Kyle's contribution for that day. Certainly it was considered sensational enough to put on the front page of the paper but, strangely, not in the most prominent position. That was occupied by another 'Exclusive' in which the paper's reporter Danny McGrory related how a guerrilla had pointed a gun at him in the Lebanon. Can it be that the paper considered a threat to one of its staff of more interest and indeed more importance than an attempt on the life of one of the superpower leaders? No, not even the *Express* is capable of such a judgment. The truth of the matter, one suspects, is that the *Express* had misgivings about the Andropov story but decided to run it because it was a 'good yarn'. Naturally the next day the rest of Fleet Street treated the whole absurd fantasy with derision, noting for the most part that Andropov's absence was due to kidney failure and its side effects. One might expect some sort of correction or gesture of atonement for the gaffe, but not a bit of it. Michael Evans, the paper's defence correspondent, was given space to confuse the *Daily Express* reader further:

> A spate of fresh rumours emerged from Moscow yesterday on the fate of the absent leader Yuri Andropov after the *Daily Express* revelations of reports that he might have been shot. The most bizarre is that the president was shot either in the arm or the leg by the wife of former interior minister Nikolai Shchlokov.

Where was Yuri Brezhnev, the man who had played such a colourful part in the previous day's story? He was at his office in a Soviet ministry, although the *Express* omitted to mention this interesting fact. Mr Evans ended his piece with a question: 'So, fact or fiction? No one will know for sure either in the West or Soviet Union.'

That too is untrue. Even in the opaque world of Russian politics everyone knew that the *Daily Express* had made an ass of itself but had not had the grace to admit it.

Presumably Messrs Kyle and Evans had something resembling a source for these fantastic speculations, but clearly it was unreliable in the extreme. So too was the informant behind a story the *Express* used in the aftermath of the Parkinson affair. Following his resignation from the Cabinet, Parkinson took his wife and family for a golfing holiday on the Algarve in Portugal, apparently at the suggestion of Denis Thatcher. It was not, perhaps, the wisest choice since the Algarve is popular with British tourists during the winter and the Parkinsons' whereabouts soon became known to the *Express* gossip column, William Hickey. One of these tourists hinted that Mrs Parkinson had been saved from drowning in the Atlantic by two boys who 'battled through the surf' to help her back to shore. The story was judged to be so good that it was promoted from the column to a prominent position in the news pages and labelled a 'William Hickey Exclusive'. By any standards it was a pretty thin piece of reporting, relying almost entirely on the witness of Antonio Costa, twelve-year-old son of a café owner, who produced some quotes in remarkably idiomatic English. He recounted the harrowing tale of the rescue:

Mr Parkinson jumped up from his table and was shouting 'Where is she? Where is she?' He ran down to the sea but he can't swim. Everyone else in the house ran down but she was too far out. We thought she would drown,' said Antonio. After the rescue the distraught former minister comforted his wife and took her back to the exclusive villa.

Other papers, not wishing to be left behind in this cruel-twist-of-fate story, reprinted it in their late editions unchecked. The next day, however, brought a gleeful exposure by the *Daily Mail*, which never loses an opportunity to rubbish the contents of its chief rival. The facts were completely wrong; Mrs Parkinson is apparently a strong swimmer, she was never in trouble and had in reality helped young Antonio to retrieve his surfboard. As an aside, the *Daily Mail* also ridiculed the *Daily Express* for a report that Miss Sara Keays, the expectant mother of Cecil Parkinson's child, had paid a visit to the House of Commons where 'she waved at friends'. At the time of this incident she was in Oman.

All reason and sense, therefore, would dictate that the story was now dead. Mrs Parkinson had denied it, a level-headed witness who was on the beach at the time had denied it and the *Daily Express* had not been able to offer further evidence in support of the William Hickey Exclusive. But reason and sense are not the strongest qualities of the *Sun*. Whatever the evidence to the contrary the gentlemen of Bouverie Street persisted in an obstinate belief in the truth of the melodrama. The next day, some ten days after the supposed incident, the *Sun* devoted its entire front page to a Picture Exclusive, a photograph of Mrs Parkinson surrounded by her 'rescuers'.

Here is the story that accompanied it:

Pale and exhausted, the wife of the disgraced Tory Cecil Parkinson leans heavily on rescuers after a holiday swimming drama. Mrs Ann Parkinson looked near to collapse as she staggered ashore to be met by her frantic husband. And last night eye-witnesses were shocked by reports that Mrs Parkinson claimed 'she was never in the slightest danger' during her ordeal. The sea drama in Portugal was witnessed by members of a British golfing party, who produced the Page One Picture. One said the ex-Tory Party Chairman's wife looked 'drawn and shattered'.

Another, engineering firm boss Bob Rhodes, said: 'She was definitely in trouble. When she came out she looked glassy-eyed and exhausted.' Bob, of Smethwick, West Midlands, said he spotted a minute figure swimming at least 800 yards out as he sat in the beach cafe at Portugal's plush Vale de Lobo. He added: 'I raised the alarm and the lads who helped her back to shore were in the water for more than ten minutes.'

The first thing that should be said about the 'Sun Picture Exclusive' is that it appears to have been taken at night. The Daily Express report, which the Sun accepted as accurate, clearly stated that the incident had taken place after the Parkinsons had lunch at a beach café. Mrs Parkinson looks a little miserable in the picture but she is certainly nowhere near 'collapse', and her 'frantic' husband appears to be having a rather jolly time. This is probably because the photograph was taken during a beach party by a member of Mr Rhodes's golfing party. It was supplied to the Sun as an interesting snap of a well-known politician, but not as evidence of Mrs Parkinson's rescue. Rhodes was highly embarrassed by its use and, more importantly, was outraged by the way in which he was quoted. He made the following observations to me: 'I made one or two enquiries because the story shown in the Express was wrong. We tried to put it right but then it got further distorted by another newspaper. So then we contacted Mrs Parkinson and explained the situation. She was very grateful.'

The Sun had paid an unsolicited fee of £400 for the photograph, which Rhodes sent to a charity of Mrs Parkinson's choice.

One of the marvels of Fleet Street is the enduring ability of journalists to believe in what they want rather than what is. The *Sun*'s 'Picture Exclusive' is a good example. A better one is the wholesale self-delusion that took place after the prosecution of a 48-year-old debt collector for having sexual intercourse with a young girl. What captured the interest of the newspaper reporters was the revelation that the girl had been prescribed the pill at the age of ten by the Brook Advisory Centre. The *Daily Mail*, which appears to have recently elected itself the protector of Britain's youth, led the way with a front page story:

A shocked and angry couple last night demanded an inquiry into why their daughter was put on the pill at the age of ten.

The *News of the World* talked of 'scandalised MPs calling for a change in the law to stop girls as young as ten being given the pill', and the *Daily Star* asked on behalf of the mother, 'Why did they do this to my little baby?' The extensive coverage and even the demands that the government should cut its grant to the Brook Advisory Centre might have been justified if, in fact, the girl had been ten. But this was not the case. She was thirteen when she first visited the clinic and although this essential detail was made available to the newspapers by the director of the Brook Advisory Centre, the national press was determined that the girl should remain a ten-year-old. Paul Foot exposed this ludicrous behaviour on the Granada TV programme *What the Papers Say*. He found one cutting from the *Daily Mail* in which the headline maintained the girl was ten and the fifth paragraph of the story announced that she was thirteen – as he said, 'Fantasy is proclaimed in the headlines and the correcting facts are relegated to the final paragraphs.' One such paragraph in the very basement of a *Daily Telegraph* story argues that the girl's age was immaterial and that her case was still deplorable. If this was so one wonders why Fleet Street had felt the need to exaggerate in the first place. The answer, of course, is that a ten-year-old girl on the pill is a damn sight more newsworthy than a thirteen-year-old girl on the pill; the newspapers were not remotely concerned about the corrupting effects of an early visit to the family planning clinic but were simply making the most of a sensational story. And in the frequent retelling of the lurid details of the GIRL TEMPTRESS IN SEX CASE (*Daily Telegraph*) there is no small measure of prurience.

The importance that newspapers attach to pictures came home to me when, as a thoroughly inept junior reporter on a provincial daily, I was sent to interview the relatives of a young man who had been killed while competing in the Isle of Man TT races. His mother was too dazed to tell me to leave and, instead, made a pot of tea and talked about everything except the death of her son. During the half hour that I sat listening to her, a reporter from a local news agency arrived and was also invited in. After a few words of condolence he came straight to the point and asked if she had any photographs of her son and whether he could borrow them. Surprisingly she gave him an album which featured her son, his motorbike and girlfriend. With a few more pleasantries and an assurance that the album would be returned the reporter departed, leaving me to wonder if I should have made a similar request. The next day when my inadequate interview appeared and the northern editors of national newspapers carried a range of poignant snaps, it was made clear to me that I should have.

Newspapers will go to practically any lengths to acquire an arresting picture, for they make the product live and in the tabloid press provide the basic structure of the layout. They are also immensely influential in the readership's understanding of the news, a fact which seems to go unrecognised by the public and, to an extent, the Press Council. One has only to consider the much-used picture of Michael Foot hobbling along on a bleak day with a small dog and walking stick to see how damaging they can be. It was taken shortly before the general election of 1983 and was a gift to newspapers wishing to portray him as a tired, rather frail relic of the old Labour Party, particularly when Mrs Thatcher was projecting a vigorous, resolute image of herself.

It is odd that the Press Council does not address itself more to the pictorial element of newspapers. A few complaints are received each year but these are generally made on grounds of intrusion or bad taste, as in the disgraceful picture printed by the *Sun* during the last months of David Niven's terminal illness. There are, however, other occasions which would seem to merit the attention of the Council, especially when newspapers use pictures which distort the truth or lie.

The *Daily Star*, in common with every newspaper, possesses a quite unnatural obsession with the vagaries of the British climate. During the unusually hot spell in the summer of '83 picture editors soon exhausted the stock ideas of 'tiny tots paddling' and 'Page Three lovelies' stripping off under garden hoses and the like. The *Daily Star*'s solution to the vexed problem of showing exactly how hot it was was to dispatch a photographer with instructions to crack an egg over the bonnet of a taxi and immortalise the sizzling result with his camera. Presumably some historically-minded soul on the paper had remembered that General Montgomery's desert army had cooked its egg rations on tank turrets. But while the trick may have worked in the Sahara it was altogether a failure in Manchester. Each time the photographer cracked an egg the mucus ran down the bonnet creating, one imagines, an unappealing mess. Newspaper photographers are a resourceful and determined bunch, however, and this one went in search of a joke shop where he rightly calculated that he would be able to buy a plastic imitation fried egg. He placed it on the bonnet of another taxi, the picture was taken and the thoroughly convincing proof of the heatwave was duly published.

My attempts to confirm this surreal behaviour, or even to trace the cutting, met with little success until in the guise of one Roger Walker I wrote to Lloyd Turner. I claimed to have had a bet with a friend that it was possible to fry an egg on the bonnet of a car. The 'proof' duly arrived in the shape of the cutting and a delighted note from the editor's secretary.

The *Sun*, unsurprisingly, leads the way in pictorial deception. For a period during the 'bingo war' of 1983 the paper demonstrated its skills at tampering with photographs in a series of highly entertaining features entitled 'Great Moments in Bingo History'. My favourite was the picture of the Russian Politburo all voting with one hand and holding Sun bingo cards with the other (the caption read, 'Sun Bingo gets everyone's vote comrades. Even in the Kremlin Russia's top politicians are on their Marx to Chekhov their numbers'). One assumed that even the *Sun*'s readership were not taken in by this, but they will certainly have been fooled by a picture of Dennis Nilsen, the homosexual murderer of Muswell Hill. On November 4 the Scottish *Daily Record* published a photograph of Nilsen, taken when he was in the army, showing him cutting a large hunk of meat with a knife. The next day the *Sun* published the same picture; now, however, Nilsen wielded, not a knife, but a menacing meat-cleaver, placed in his hand by someone in the paper's photographic process department.

This department's expertise in touching-up and marrying pictures together is unequalled in Fleet Street. Even as I write the *Sun* is exposed by one of its rivals for the results of their deft craftsmanship. It seems that prior to the marriage of the pop star Elton John the paper determined that the identity and the appearance of his bride was of considerable public interest. The picture desk tried for several days to acquire a photograph of her, but none was available; so it decided on the simple expedient of picking a likely looking bride from the picture library and inserting her at the singer's side in a single print. Needless to say, she had never had any connection with Elton John. The process department's greatest triumph was when the Princess of Wales attended a gala evening in a fairly low-cut dress. There was some debate in Fleet Street as to whether the Princess was exposing rather too much of the Royal bust; however, the pictures printed in the national press the next day proved that she was as demure and decent as ever. But the *Sun* photographer appeared to have got a better view than the other photographers since his picture included dark hints of the Princess's nipples. This struck his rivals as strange since they were quite sure that they had all had exactly the same position. It was also unlikely this particular group of gentlemen would fail to spot such a wonderfully appealing picture. The explanation of course was that the nipples had been painted into the picture by the process department.

The *Sun* is also good at reconstructing incidents that its photographers have missed. One of the paper's reporters was sent to interview Dr Robert Jones, a GP in Essex whose wife was murdered and who, as a result, endured more newspaper harassment than perhaps anyone else during 1983. With the appearance of this particular reporter, who, curiously, was the paper's education correspondent, Dr Jones's patience gave in and he poured a large bucket of water on his head. The man telephoned the news to his office in London and retired to a local pub to dry his clothes and drown his sorrows. His day was not yet over, however; as Peter Tory of the *Daily Mirror* recorded, 'he was dragged outside the pub and for the benefit of the paper's photographer had another bucket of water thrown at him by a colleague acting strictly under instructions from the *Sun*.'

On November 9 the *Sun* felt that its readers should like to be acquainted with the story of Jane Patey. Under the headline SPIDER IN CAR MADE THIS MISS MUFFETT we are told by Phil Dampier:

Pretty Jane Patey wrecked her car . . . because a spider sat down beside her. Like Little Miss Muffett Jane took fright and swerved after the tiny little beastie 'dropped from the windscreen to her lap'. . . . 'I know it's ridiculous, but I'm terrified of spiders. They just scare me stiff. It wasn't even a very big spider, just a fairly small one.'

Accompanying the story was a large picture of the glamorous Jane, captioned 'YUK . . . terrified Jane examines the spider that sat down beside her. It caused her to crash her car.' And, there, indeed, was the spider sitting quietly on her shoulder for the benefit of Haydn Jones, the photographer. Odd that, having crashed her car from arachnophobic fright, she does not exhibit the least bit of fear in the picture; odder still that while she said it was 'just a fairly small' spider, the creature on her shoulder would do justice to an Amazonian rain forest. In fact the spider came neither from the tropics nor from Jane's battered mini, but from a joke shop in Taunton. 'The man from the *Sun* had to come all the way from Bristol because he had to stop off and buy a plastic spider. I think he couldn't find a shop which sold them,' Miss Patey said a few days after she had occupied the whole of Page Five in a national newspaper.

There is absolutely no shame attached to being responsible for these activities. In many cases the good operator will boast of the deception to his colleagues; such wheezes are generally applauded and enter the bar-room mythology of Fleet Street. It is often difficult to see the point of them. While the news that Andropov had been 'shot' may conceivably have sold more copies of the *Daily Express*, it is hard to imagine a single copy being sold as a result of joke spiders and bogus fried eggs.

CHAPTER 3

The Fun-Loving Royals

A French newspaper editor once conducted a survey of the way in which the French press presented the British Royal Family, and came up with the following set of statistics. Between 1958 and 1972 the Queen was pregnant ninety-two times, had 149 accidents and nine miscarriages and took the pill eleven times. She abdicated sixty-three times and was on the point of breaking up with Prince Philip seventy-three times. She was said to be fed up 112 times and on the verge of a nervous breakdown thirty-two times. She had forty-three unhappy nights, twenty-seven nightmares, and her life was threatened twenty-nine times. She was rude to the Queen of Persia eleven times, to Princess Grace of Monaco six times and to Queen Fabiola only twice; and she expelled Lord Snowdon from Court 151 times. A survey of the British press over the last five years, a golden era of creativity among Fleet Street's royal correspondents, would not produce such a high level of incident, but it certainly gives an alarming picture of the Royal Family's lifestyle. The Princess of Wales, for instance, has been pregnant at least four times; she has suffered numerous bouts of the slimmers' disease anorexia nervosa and a severe case of post-natal depression. She has had countless violent rows with her husband, the Queen, Prince Philip and Princess Anne, and she is constantly being ticked off for misbehaviour during formal occasions. Prince Charles has more or less been ignored since his wedding, but his brother Andrew has been credited with a tally of conquests which would exceed the reasonable expectations of any man's lifetime. Meanwhile, Captain

Mark Phillips has been on the point of leaving his 'headstrong' wife Princess Anne on several occasions. Or was it the other way round? At any rate Angela Rippon, the BBC newscaster who shares his passion for horses, was hinted by the press to have found other common interests with him. And so it goes on, fabrication on top of fantasy based on rumour and wishful thinking.

King George VI is said to have been amused by Fleet Street's flights of fancy and to have made a hobby of compiling a book of press cuttings entitled 'Things My Daughter Never Did'. Since his death Buckingham Palace Press Office has occasionally attempted to log inaccuracies with a view to demonstrating to the national press its appalling record. But the exercise always proved too time-consuming and depressing and was abandoned in the knowledge that journalists were unlikely to be weaned from their extravagant habits.

Fleet Street royalty-watchers are peculiarly unfettered by the restraints that apply in all other fields of journalistic endeavour. The Royal Family has only once this century resorted to the libel laws in response to a damaging fabrication and it is unlikely to do so again. The Press Office rarely issues categoric denials on the grounds that it is not always in full possession of the facts and a refusal to deny a story outright will be read as confirmation. Michael Shea, the Queen's Press Secretary since 1978, has, in fact, been goaded into denying stories only twice in the eight years he has held the post. The first was the *Daily Express*'s confident assertion that Prince Charles was to marry Princess Marie Astrid of Luxembourg; the second was the *Sunday Mirror*'s 'revelation' that he had arranged for the Royal Train to stop on a remote part of the British Rail network so that his future bride, Lady Diana Spencer, could join him for a romantic night in the sidings. On both occasions the press persisted in the belief that it knew better and used the Palace denials to maintain interest in the stories. This lack of restraint gives journalists considerable license, but in the last two years the Queen has determined that their intrusion into her family's privacy should not go further.

In 1981 she summoned all newspaper editors to the Palace and asked them to stop harassing the Princess of Wales, who was being driven to distraction by the paparazzi (freelance photographers who specialise in private pictures of the famous at play). This civilised meeting was marred by two Murdoch editors: Barry Askew, then editor of the *News of the World*, cheekily delivered himself of the view that the press had a right to cover Princess Di whether she was attending a film première or buying wine gums. At the last moment Kelvin Mackenzie of the *Sun* refused the invitation altogether, sending a message to Michael Shea indicating that he deemed a meeting with his proprietor to be more important. The meeting also included a request that the Royal Family should be left to enjoy their annual winter holiday at Sandringham in privacy. The editors returned to Fleet Street presumably with good intentions, but old habits die hard. They were soon giving as much space as always to the Princess, and by Christmas 1983 the Queen again had to deliver a stern rebuke for the intrusion at Sandringham.

Privacy, or at least a measure of it, seems to be her overriding concern. Fabrications and downright lies have, apparently, long since ceased to bother her and her family. To this end the Queen instigated legal proceedings against Kieran Kenny, a minor Royal servant who knowingly broke an agreement forbidding him communicate with the press during and after his employment at Buckingham Palace. He sold his story to the *Sun*, which published a centre-page spread headlined THE ASTONISHING SECRETS OF THE FUN LOVING ROYALS – KOO'S ROMPS AT THE PALACE. The Queen won her action without going to court and the Press Council some six months later condemned the *Sun* for failing to make adequate enquiries about Kenny's legal obligations to the Palace and, more importantly, for invading the Royal Family's privacy. During the Press Council hearing, Mackenzie again had pressing business elsewhere, but he said, through the paper's legal manager, Henry Douglas, that 'affection and loyalty for our Royals was sustained by the unceasing publicity about their lives'. Mackenzie was being less than frank. Although the sentiment is frequently used to justify saturation coverage, the real reason for this unceasing publicity is that Royal stories sell newspapers, however lightly they sit with the truth, and this, of course, was uppermost in Mackenzie's mind when he began to run Kenny's dubious material.

The Royal family, together with bingo and television soap operas, is currently the subject of the most intense competition among popular newspapers. At one stage during 1982, the *Daily Mirror* and *Sun* pursued a policy of using a front-page Royal story every Monday, traditionally the day when Fleet Street launches a weekly drive for increased sales. It goes without saying that the first requirement of these Monday leads was not accuracy. All that was asked of the Royal correspondents was for a suitably sensational snippet to kick off the week.

James Whitaker, formerly of the *Express* Group and now the *Daily Mirror*'s Royal expert, is the doyen of this unlovely group. He takes himself and his job very seriously and is frequently to be seen on television authoritatively holding forth on every aspect of the Royal Family. Although Whitaker earns his considerable living from a thoroughly working-class organ, he affects the manner and dress of a country gentleman. He has an engaging smile and the ruddy complexion of a man who rides to hounds at least twice a week. This is more due to the many hours that he has spent in all weathers stalking various Royal estates in the hope of catching sight of a member of the family, particularly Princess Diana, with whom he boasts a near mystical understanding. Whitaker's rivals are Ashley Walton at the *Daily Express*, Stephen Lynas at the *Daily Mail* and until recently Harry Arnold at the *Sun*. But by common consent Whitaker leads the field, and it is in recognition of his pre-eminence that I produce an Exclusive from the front page of the *Daily Mirror* of September 17, 1983.

'Princess Diana is expecting her second baby, according to Buckingham Palace sources,' he announced to the world some three months before the Princess actually conceived for the second time. This remarkable prescience seems to have been inspired by one of Whitaker's legion of loose-tongued informants in the household. (Buckingham Palace, incidentally, strongly doubts whether his sources are as good as he claims.) However:

She is said to have passed on the good news at a dinner party at Balmoral Castle two weeks ago. This was after she met her gynaecologist, Mr George Pinker, in London. The Royal Family were delighted and called for champagne to celebrate. I am told, 'There was a lot of kissing at the same time, followed by a very jolly dinner party.'

These few lines amount to the only evidence that Whitaker could produce to support the confident assertion of the first paragraph. Towards the end of the story he helpfully explained why his rivals had not got hold of it: 'The intention has been to protect her from the enormous amount of publicity that is bound to follow any official announcement.'

In fact, the publicity that followed the announcement of her real pregnancy months later was rather mild and certainly did not justify his anxieties. Whitaker had gone through the motions of checking the story with Buckingham Palace, mentioning along the way that he had been visited by a strong and mysterious conviction in the matter. As usual Michael Shea did not deny the story, but he did try to persuade him from following his instincts. He might have saved himself the bother; Whitaker then claimed: 'Even Buckingham Palace Press Officers have not been told that the Princess is pregnant.'

The *Daily Mirror* has of late been striking a self-righteous pose towards its rival, the *Sun*. Mike Molloy, the editor, should perhaps cast his mind back to the events in his newsroom on November 11, 1983, which led to a Front Page Exclusive by Edward Vale. The first thing to make clear about this story is that Mr Vale bears no responsibility for its contents.

Headlined DIANA AND THE LITTLE OLD LADY, it began:

Princess Diana regularly visits an elderly woman who lives in a tiny terraced house. It is one of Diana's best kept secrets and she looked taken aback when she was spotted leaving the house in a London suburb yesterday. She said, 'I have been to see an old lady friend.' The detective walked with her towards the black painted front door which was unlocked, Diana pushed it open and closed it behind her.

It is an indication of how little the *Mirror* had in the way of information that it actually described the Princess opening the door. Anyway, the story was intriguing enough and left readers with the impression that the Princess had charitably kept up visits to some lonely old pensioner. It came to the paper from one of the paparazzi and was written up on the instructions of the news desk while Edward Vale was dispatched to check such details as there were and discover the identity of the little old lady. He reported back that he could do little to substantiate the photographer's story and said that he thought it should not be published. Unfortunately for him, the news editor and editor had already determined that it was precisely the sort of lead they wanted for a Saturday morning; moreover, his name would be on top of it.

That weekend brought a contemptuous exposure by the *News of the World* which correctly reported that the Princess had been attending dancing classes in a studio in Chiswick, as the *News of the World* had recorded some weeks before. And the little old lady? That, presumably, was forty-six-year-old Merle Park, the ballerina who runs the studio. The *Daily Mirror* looked extremely foolish, particularly in its use of Princess Diana's 'quote'.

Newspapers really should learn not to place so much confidence in the evidence of photographers, who often seem to suffer hallucinations when engaged on Royal stories. For lack of anything better to do in the silly season, a number of them were deployed to identify and take photographs of the people who were staying with the Royal Family for the traditional summer holiday at Balmoral. The result was that on August 22 most national dailies carried a picture of a glamorous girl who was unanimously presented as the 'new love in Andy's life'. She was Miss Sophie Birdwood, the nineteen-year-old daughter of Baron Birdwood of Anzac and of Totnes. She had been educated at Cheltenham Ladies' College, elected Deb of the Year in 1982 and had been seeing Prince Andrew on an intimate basis for some time. In their enthusiasm to find the replacement for Koo Stark, who had by that time fallen in the affections of the Prince, newspapers did not bother to check the facts with Buckingham Palace, with Miss Birdwood or her family. Here is the *Daily Mirror*:

Ex-deb, Sophie Birdwood, is being tipped as the new girl in

Prince Andrew's life after spending the weekend at Balmoral. Sophie, a slim 5ft 8ins, is a stylish dresser just like the Princess of Wales. When she was seen at Balmoral many of the Royal photographers mistook her for the Princess. A close friend said last night, 'It would not surprise me at all if Prince Andrew had fallen for her'.

Here is the *Daily Star*:

Sophie slept through the 30-minute flight from Aberdeen and tried to slip through the airport without being seen. But *Star* photographer Julian Parker, who was on the plane, remembered her as an old flame of Andrew's and Sophie whispered to her minder, 'Oh dear, he's recognised me.'

The *Daily Mail* joined in the fun, but was not quite so definite when it came to linking Miss Birdwood and Prince Andrew: 'As nineteen-year-old Sophie returned home to Sloane Square, London, Royal observers were wondering who had invited her to Balmoral.'

It is not often that Fleet Street is made to look so gratifyingly stupid; egg was liberally spread from one end to the other. For the very next day Sophie Birdwood landed at Heathrow after a long holiday in the Bahamas, and even the dimmest reporters saw that she could not possibly have been on the Aberdeen flight the day before. They had, of course, got the wrong girl. Or, rather, published the picture of the right girl but with the wrong name. The girl they had met off the Aberdeen flight was the Honourable Carolyn Herbert, the twenty-one-year-old daughter of the Queen's racing manager, Lord Porchester, who had been invited to Balmoral by the Princess of Wales, not Prince Andrew. All of which proved not a little unsettling for the reporter who had waxed knowledgably on Miss Birdwood's close ties with Prince Andrew. One wonders where the *Daily Mirror* found this 'close friend' and indeed whether they had not just made him or her up altogether. Certainly the close friend seemed remarkably ignorant about Miss Birdwood's life. It is interesting to note, after such a monumental gaffe, that only the *Daily Mail* had the grace to apologise to Sophie, Carolyn and Andrew. The other newspapers corrected the story by recounting the whole mix-up as if they had all been innocent observers.

The nearest Fleet Street comes to having anything like a reliable Buckingham Palace source is usually a member of the household like Kieran Kenny who is disaffected or simply tempted by large amounts of money to break the pledge of confidentiality. Michelle Riles, a twenty-three-year-old Yorkshire girl, left her job as maid on Friday and by the Saturday was offering 'The sensational Upstairs, Downstairs story of her experiences in the Royal service' to the *News of the World*. Clearly it was not a very impressive one since, instead of buying it, the paper compiled a story on how Miss Riles came to be selling it, and very enlightening it was too. She had written a fan letter to one Christopher Hutchins, who runs a gossip column for the *Sunday Mirror*. It seems that she had been struck by Hutchins's resemblance to a detective working for the Royal Family. Some years ago, Hutchins achieved a certain notoriety by revealing the indiscretions of the singers Tom Jones and Engelbert Humperdinck, whom he had represented as publicity agent. He is not one to pass off the opportunity of a good source at Buckingham Palace. He followed up the letter and in due course put it to her that she should leave Buckingham Palace and write a book with him on her experiences there. He said that there would be a lot of money in it for her and placed the sale in the hands of New York agent Lucianne Goldberg, who immediately offered it to the *News of the World*.

Whether the paper ever had any intention of using the story is doubtful since the Palace had let it be known that it would do everything in its power to stop publication. However two reporters, Polly Hepburn and Sara Rust, listened to what Hutchins had to say. He asked £30,000 for the basic version of Miss Riles's story, an incredible amount but doubtless well within the *News of the World*'s capabilities. The piece that actually appeared in the paper must have come as something of a shock to Hutchins and Riles; he was described as a worm, and the maid was, with the help of a long interview with her mother, Sandra Riles, made to look a silly, rather impressionable girl. No doubt all this proved embarrassing for Hutchins not only personally but professionally too, since it must have looked odd to his employers at the *Sunday Mirror* that he was trying to sell a story to their main rival.

It ill behoves the *News of the World*, never the most virtuous of newspapers, to expose the activities of characters like Hutchins. Still, a good purpose is served if the negotiations which precede the publication of these scoops are revealed.

Another Royal servant who came to the attention of the press was Andrew Lightwood, Princess Anne's butler at Gatcombe Park. It was never really clear if Mr Lightwood planned to sell his story or not. On one hand he swore blind that nothing could buy his loyalty to the Royal Family; on the other, certain foreign magazines were offered what James Whitaker, no less, described as 'an extremely sordid story which dealt exclusively with the homosexual mafia in the Buckingham Palace household'.

It was the manner of Lightwood's leaving that first engaged the interest of the press. William Hickey led the way with an impressive news story on the front page of the *Express* for December 8:

> Royal butler Andrew Lightwood has been forced to give up his job with Princess Anne and go into hiding after a series of death threat phone calls. The caller, speaking with a pronounced Irish accent, used an unlisted number for Gatcombe Park, the Princess' Gloucestershire home. On each occasion the man asked for Lightwood by name. And the message was 'we are going to kill you . . . ' He gave his notice to Princess Anne and fled to stay with relatives in South Wales. From there yesterday he said, 'Princess Anne, whom I like very much, was sympathetic and understood my fears. She was concerned for my safety and police took the calls seriously'.

The key part of the story, and the one which caused considerable alarm at Buckingham Palace and at Scotland Yard, was 'speaking with a pronounced Irish accent'. It left no doubt that Lightwood had been subject to some sort of threat from the I.R.A. And it caused particular concern because the police had already received intelligence that the I.R.A. was planning a new offensive on the British mainland. Why Lightwood, a rather junior and unimportant member of the household, should be threatened was a mystery. There was no explanation to be found in the William Hickey story. The police questioned Lightwood and found that somewhere along the line the number of calls he had actually received was exaggerated from two to fourteen and, more important, he denied saying that the caller had a heavy Irish accent and asked for him by name. Where this came from one cannot say, but the other papers followed it up and the Irish caller became an established fact even though Buckingham Palace tried to correct it. Eventually, to prevent any further misunderstanding, lawyers acting for Princess Anne got a court order instructing Lightwood, who does seem to have been unusually free with his comments, to comply with the pledge of confidentiality.

Here one has been forced to equivocate; the truth of the matter is simply not clear. All one can say is that Lightwood was *not* threatened by a caller with an Irish accent. There are no doubts, however, about the *Daily Express*'s revelation that the Duchess of Kent would enter hospital in July 1983 to receive electro-convulsive therapy. It was malicious and senseless fabrication on the scale of the *Sun*'s 'interview' with Mrs Marica McKay. Its prominence in the paper may not have been so great, but it did rely on the distress of the subject and was used in the knowledge that the Duchess was unlikely to sue or to complain to the Press Council. Again the story was a 'William Hickey Exclusive', promoted from the gossip column to the news pages:

> The Duchess of Kent is to enter a London hospital in the next few days for a new and extensive course of treatment. She has been unwell since an operation for the removal of an ovarian cyst in April. Officials at the King Edward VII hospital for officers say the Duchess, 50, will now undergo further tests which will be followed by treatment for the depression which has haunted her since her miscarriage in 1977. I understand the treatment may include electro-convulsive therapy, a controversial method of tackling extreme depression which can affect the memory. Should such a step be taken, it is likely that the Duchess's public career could be over for some considerable time. It already seems certain that she will be unable to undertake any further engagements this year. Medical experts believe it is possible that her public life, with the exception of a few brief appearances, is over for ever.

Now, let us consider this in some detail. The first thing to say is that the electro-convulsive therapy is only introduced in the third paragraph of the story. If William Hickey really knew what he was talking about, this information, which after all is the point of the story, would have appeared in the first line. Second, this crucial paragraph opens with the words, 'I understand', which in the code of the gossip columnist means, 'I have heard a vague rumour, I am unable to confirm it but I am going to use the story anyway.' Third, this Hickey Exclusive provides no supporting evidence that the Duchess is going to receive the treatment, it neither quotes a hospital spokesman, nor the Duchess's press secretary, Sir Richard Buckley. Fourth, the Duchess was far from being unable to undertake any further engagements during 1983. Within a matter of weeks she took part in a singing festival at King's Lynn in Norfolk. Fifth, Hickey mentioned near the end of the story that the Duchess was being 'attended by a full-time nurse on a 24-hour-a-day basis'. She had no nurse, not even on a part-time basis.

This then was an unsubstantiated gossip paragraph, inflated by innuendo and circumstantial detail to occupy a sizable spot on the news page. The projection of the story would have undoubtedly left the readership with a firm understanding that the Duchess of Kent was so ill that she was to receive the dangerous and largely discredited treatment.

The next day's papers unanimously poured scorn on the story. The *Daily Telegraph* interviewed Sir Richard Buckley, who denounced it as a 'total and thoroughly unkind fabrication'. He also expressed his astonishment that the paper had never consulted him before using the story. The *Daily Mirror* sought out the Duchess's daughter, Lady Helen Windsor, who said, 'It was nonsense, my mother is merely a little tired.' At the same time the *Express* was made fully aware of the facts in a telephone call from Sir Richard to Lord Matthews, the Chairman of Express Newspapers. It seems to have had little effect and the next day the paper published the following odious self-justification under the headline, ON THE SIDE OF THE DUCHESS:

A spokesman for the Duchess of Kent leapt into print yesterday with the suggestion that my story about the Duchess's illness was unkind and a total fabrication.

The *Daily Express* explicitly rejects both suggestions. Far from being unkind, this newspaper has been deeply concerned about the health of the Duchess and recognises that her health is a matter of considerable concern to many people.

Over many years the *Express* has applauded the Duchess's devotion to duty and has recognised her for the charming and dedicated person she undoubtedly is.

The suggestion that my story was a fabrication is not merely wrong, but outrageous. The *Daily Express* does not fabricate stories. What I reported was that the Duchess was expected to enter hospital for treatment for her nervous disorder and that the treatment may entail ECT – electro-convulsive therapy.

The sources for this story are impeccable. On this occasion I am confident that the *Daily Express* is better informed than the Duchess's spokesman.

It is hard to imagine a more arrogant and unconvincing piece of hypocrisy. The most offensive part of it was the way in which the spurious concern for the Duchess's health was woven into a reiteration of the original claim, a claim which the *Express* felt there was no need to support by further evidence.

An apology was what was needed, but it is an indication of the popular press's considerable estimation of its own authority that editors so strongly resist the insertion of apologies or correcting information. If they do appear it is usually the result of legal action, a course which was not really open to the Duchess, and even then they are buried away so that only a fraction of the readership sees them. A good example of this is the way in which the ALL EXCLUSIVE NO. 1 SUN of December 7, 1983, handled the huge mistake of the ALL EXCLUSIVE NO. 1 SUN of December 6, 1983.

The first story, 'Another Sun Exclusive', was headlined EDWARD BANNED FROM PUB:

Student Prince Edward has been booted out of a pub by the landlord – a retired Guards Sergeant-Major.

Ex-RSM Peter Adams gave the Prince and five college chums their marching orders for interrupting a crucial darts match.

The student revellers were on a fun run, downing half pints in a succession of pubs – when they burst into the 150-year-old Bakers Arms in Cambridge.

Landlady, Helen Adams, warned them to stop giggling and larking about. Mr Adams, 6ft tall, greasy haired and still with a ramrod straight back said yesterday, 'We will not have riffraff in here.'

Kieran Saunders, the author of this extraordinary story, quoted the RSM's wife as saying, 'An older man in a green anorak was with them and he came to apologise to me. He could have been the Prince's detective.'

Exactly the same account appeared in later editions of the *Daily Star* under Sidney Brennan's byline. Clearly he had made no checks either, which proved embarrassing the next day when a young BBC engineer, David Swallow, admitted organising a pub crawl in Cambridge with five friends who dressed up as Prince Edward and his friends – some two months before the *Sun* reported the story. Probably because it had not been responsible for initiating the story, the *Daily Star* printed a long and fairly detailed explanation of how the press had been hoodwinked. The *Sun*, however, is more used to such embarrassments and published a curt four sentences which explained little and regretted nothing. Clearly Prince Edward just has to put up with being a victim of Mr Mackenzie's 'affection and loyalty for our Royals'.

The front page of the *Sun* – again – for November 3 bears more than a cursory glance and could provide a useful exercise in news analysis for the various schools of journalism that have sprung up around Britain over the last decade. Aside from the grossly distorted Royal story, the most interesting aspect of the page is the linking of headlines of the three unrelated stories. Reading from the top of the page you have: SPURS FANS IN BLOODBATH; then BOOZY KIDS' PALACE RAVE UP; then LIEUT EDWARD CAPS THE LOT. The last is accompanied by a picture of Prince Edward, leaving the reader with a subliminal impression that two sets of hooligans have gone on the rampage, one of which has been led by Prince Edward.

The main story (Another Sun Exclusive) dealt with a party to mark the twenty-first anniversary of the Community Service Volunteers. Shan Lancaster wrote:

> The Queen has shared an amazing rave-up at Buckingham Palace . . . with punks, skinheads and ex-borstal kids. The boozy three-hour thrash left Palace staff buzzing with shock and excitement last night. For as the Queen, Prince Philip, Premier Margaret Thatcher and Labour Leader Neil Kinnock chatted to almost 1,000 youngsters, the antics included:
>
> GIGGLING girls sliding down the Palace banisters with glasses in their hands.
>
> A FOOTMAN in knee breeches breaking up a scuffle between two teenagers.
>
> FLOWERS and ashtrays being pocketed as souvenirs.
>
> ONE LAD, full of Palace hospitality, being sick in the courtyard. At one stage the Queen was chatting to punks with green and orange hair.

The message is clear: Things are not what they used to be at the Palace. Anarchy reigns while the Queen chats to punks and skinheads. Strange that the last four paragraphs of the story completely contradict the sensational headline and introduction. The Palace admits that the odd guest may have taken a flower for his or her buttonhole but goes on to say:

> The Queen certainly stayed until the end of the reception and the police were not called in. There were drinks on offer for those of drinking age and soft drinks as well. All I can say is that it was a very, very successful evening indeed.

The *Daily Mail* followed a similar policy, building up the story in the headline RAMPAGE AT PALACE and knocking it down in the conclusion. Interestingly it was also placed next to the story of the Spurs fans rioting in Rotterdam. Stephen Lynas wrote:

> A group of teenagers went on the rampage at a Buckingham Palace reception hosted by the Queen. As guests chatted quietly at the prestige reception, punks and skinheads went wild.

But his last two paragraphs read:

> The Queen after spending two hours at the reception had no

idea what went on. Nor had the vast majority of the guests. There is no question of the Queen being angry or saying such events should not be held in the future. There was absolutely no question of things getting out of hand.

Perhaps one or two of the thousand guests did get mildly carried away, but the coverage was out of all proportion to the incidents, which took place four days before either paper carried the story.

The serious press, while never indulging in the fantasy, sensationalism and distortion of the tabloids, does get a lot wrong about the Royal Family. The *Sunday Times*, for instance, carried a story to the effect that Princess Diana had insisted on buying a canopied four-poster bed which had belonged to Diane de Poitiers, 'whose talents as courtesan had a way of cleaving through the sixteenth-century bureaucracy'. It had cost some £110,000 but there was a delay in the export of the bed because cultural officials objected to a piece of furniture so intimately associated with French history leaving the country. A member of the *Sunday Times* staff telephoned Buckingham Palace to check the story. It was without foundation. The spokesman offered the view that the exporters of the bed had put about the rumour that it was destined for the Royal couple's home at Highclere in order to cleave a way through twentieth-century bureaucracy. Knowing this, the *Sunday Times* still published the story.

The serious newspapers also do much to raise alarm where there is none, particularly over the Queen's visits abroad or her relations with the government of the time. Take their reporting of the discussions between the Queen and Margaret Thatcher during the American invasion of Grenada. These weekly meetings are utterly secret and Prime Ministers rarely disclose in detail the topics discussed. However, the *Times* and *Sunday Times* felt themselves sufficiently well-informed to disclose that the Queen strongly disapproved of Margaret Thatcher's opposition to Reagan's action. One wonders where this idea came from, especially since the *Times* had been instructed to take a strong pro-American line by its proprietor Rupert Murdoch.

Buckingham Palace estimates that at least seventy per cent of Royal stories contain some sort of factual inaccuracy – only to be expected when so many are based on gossip from the Bag O'Nails public house, where palace servants spend their lunch-hours. The fault should partly be laid at the door of the Palace itself, which has become excessively discreet in the interests of protecting the Royal Family's privacy. Moreover, its unwillingness to deny stories seems self-defeating. Naturally the Press Office cannot always be in full possession of the facts, but it is certain that it will know a good deal more than its tormentors.

CHAPTER 4

'Damn Your Principles!

Stick to Your Party!'

Disraeli

When Mrs Thatcher announced the General Election of 1983, she and her party knew that they could confidently rely on varying degrees of support from these papers: the *Daily Mail*, the *Mail on Sunday*, the *Sun*, the *News of the World*, the *Daily Telegraph*, the *Sunday Telegraph*, the *Times*, the *Sunday Times*, the *Daily Express*, the *Sunday Express* and the *Standard*. The papers that remained committed to the Labour cause were the *Daily Mirror*, the *Sunday Mirror* and the *Sunday People*, while the *Guardian*, *Observer* and, surprisingly, the *Daily Star* maintained a more or less independent stance until polling week. Put more simply, daily papers with circulations totalling 11,400,000 supported the Conservative party, as opposed to the combined circulation of 3,650,000 of papers that put an alternative view. The Sunday market was split in favour of the Conservatives 10,127,000 to 7,585,500.

There is nothing new in this. The bias has been a fact of political life since the Labour party first emerged as the Conservatives' chief competitor. There have been periods when the left and independent voices have had a larger audience, but during the Thatcher years the concensus of newspaper opinion has been greater than at any time since Clement Attlee's post-war government. The bias, of course, exhibits itself in the perfectly acceptable quarters of editorial columns but it also appears in the news pages, particularly in the tabloid press, where opinion is woven into what are presented as factual reports. There is nothing new in this either, although again there seems to have been an increase in politically opinionated news stories in the last five years.

There are plenty of extreme manifestations of this bias in the reporting of politics during 1983, though it is not always easy to spot who is actually responsible. For while journalists can be unreliable in matters of truth, unscrupulous in propagating their own convictions and ready to omit, distort and dissemble with some political expedient in mind, they are matched point for point by the subject matter, that is to say politicians.

If ever there appeared to be a clear case of politically motivated fabrication, it was the steady insistence of the Conservative press in the first four months of 1983 that Michael Foot would resign as leader of the Labour party. For the previous three years Fleet Street had, with unconcealed glee, covered the hostility and divisions engendered in the Labour party by the reforms of the Bennite left. From a Labour view these predictions were explained as a crude attempt to keep these rifts fully exposed for the coming general election and thus create the impression that Mrs Thatcher's was the only party fit to be entrusted with the nation's destiny. The strongest stories appeared in the week preceding the Bermondsey by-election, when it was clear that the Labour candidate, Peter Tatchell, stood little chance of retaining a Labour stronghold. The *Daily Mail*'s political editor Gordon Greig floated the idea on the front page of the paper that Labour MPs would accept a return to James Callaghan as leader. He stated that Foot's future relied on the support of three union leaders, Moss Evans of the transport workers, David Basnett of the municipal workers and the ubiquitous Clive Jenkins of the managerial staff union. He concluded the story thus:

> The question that no one in the socialist hierarchy is prepared
> to answer at the moment is: Who will wield the knife if Bermond-
> sey does turn out to be a disaster?
>
> At Westminster the hope is that the unions will do it. But has
> Basnett, Evans or Jenkins got the nerve?

The reply to this came in the *Sunday Telegraph*, which quoted Sam McCluskey, a union leader and then chairman of the Labour party, who dismissed the rumours as 'mischievous and unfounded'. And Foot himself, drawing parallels with the Zinoviev letter, which the Labour party still blames for its defeat in 1924, observed that rumours had chiefly appeared in the *Mail*, the *Times*, the *Sun* and the *Daily Express*, all newspapers that strongly opposed his election as leader in the first place. He added that Denis Healey had publicly declared his loyalty and confidence in the leadership. Here, then, would seem to be the perfect example of the Tory press sowing the seeds of discord in the Shadow Cabinet and unions. Although Foot had quickly exposed this, it would appear that they were unrestrained in their malice towards him. When the Bermondsey result was duly announced at the end of the week Anthony Bevins, formerly of the *Daily Mail* and now a political correspondent for the *Times*, led the paper with the following story:

> The majority of Labour's shadow cabinet including some of those who have previously expressed the belief that Michael Foot should stay on as leader now feel that he should go.
>
> Hostility to Mr Foot is now strong among Labour MPs and in the Shadow Cabinet key parliamentary sources believe that Dennis Healey will take over as leader within the next month.
>
> Over the past seven days it has been impossible to find a Labour MP who will state that Mr Foot will lead the party into the next general election. The despair and depression themselves are sapping the fight and strength of the party.

He went on to explain that Mr Kinnock would be a likely deputy and the resultant Healey—Kinnock ticket would receive the firm support of the unions. This brought an unequivocal reaction from Foot, who was quoted in the next issue of the *Times* by another political reporter, Philip Webster, as saying:

> I regard the story in the *Times* as malicious fabrication. It could be based on some tittle tattle from a few people talking. I have plenty of evidence that confirms my view that it is the desire of the party that I should stay. Not a single Shadow Cabinet minister has spoken to me in the sense described in the *Times*. Since they are honourable men I am sure they would have done so if they had felt that way.
>
> What the *Times* and the Conservative party want is to keep the

divisions in the party on the boil all the time in the headlines. That is the way they think they can cause the maximum injury to the party.

During the month of March, which included the Labour victory at Darlington, the stories disappeared, giving the lie, one supposed, to the unsourced rumour and speculation of February. A selection of headlines from the *Times* would seem to confirm the impression that Foot had shamed Fleet Street into more honest journalism: MORE BACKING FOR FOOT AS LEADER, MORE UNION SUPPORT FOR FOOT, CHAPPLE SAYS FOOT MUST STAY ON and UNIONS UNITE UNDER FOOT. But come April, the rumour-mongers were at it again, reporting that the union leaders were plotting and that the Parliamentary Labour party were dissatisfied with Foot's ratings in the polls. The stories continued unabated into May, even after the date of the general election was announced. Here is the *Daily Telegraph*'s Nicholas Comfort writing under the headline FOOT SAYS I WILL NOT QUIT, in the second week of the election campaign:

> Confronted by opinion polls showing Labour as far behind the Conservatives with Alliance fortunes reviving, Mr Foot said that the party's campaign was 'going well' and that 'he would not dream of resigning as leader at this stage'.

Even the *Guardian*, which is accepted to be among the fairest of newspapers during election time, appeared to depart from its honourable cause by assuming the Conservatives would win. Here is James Wightman writing:

> Some politicians are already predicting another outbreak of Left-versus-Right feuding over who should succeed the 69-year-old Foot should Labour lose the election. Mr Healey would be expected to be among the challengers.

Thus was the campaign against Mr Foot subtly co-ordinated until the polling booths closed on June 9. The results of it were plain to see. Foot's leadership, in turn portrayed as senile, incompetent, indecisive and querulous, became one of the election issues on which the voters of Britain decided to opt for Mrs Thatcher. Labour lost the election and, as if bound to fulfil the prophesies of all those months, Foot resigned –

in other words a *prima facie* case of journalistic intervention in the political life of the nation. Who could blame him for devoting a large portion of his farewell speech at the Labour party conference in Brighton to the abysmal behaviour of Fleet Street?

> In my opinion the debasement of journalism is worse in Fleet Street today than at any time that I can recall. . . . The bad drives out the good, the evil drives out the shoddy, the tenth rate drives out the second or third rate.

Maybe he was right in general terms, but as far as the leadership stories were concerned he had no real cause for complaint. Although of course it suited Conservative interests that his leadership was so palpably inept, the stories he and his supporters described as 'malicious fabrication, lies and unfounded mischief' were in fact largely true. If anything the national press had been slow in picking up the dissatisfaction of various figures in the Labour movement. The first real anxieties emerged at the Labour Party Conference in Blackpool in the autumn of 1982. Foot defended his position but there was renewed debate in the Christmas holiday of that year which continued through the first months of 1983.

Gordon Greig was right when he said the decision lay in the hands of the union leaders, although he may have been a trifle carried away in the speculation that ponderous old Jim Callaghan might be on the way back. Anthony Bevins was also pretty near the mark when he wrote after the Bermondsey defeat that the Shadow Cabinet was doubtful about the efficacy of Foot's leadership in election year. These stories were supported by strong guidance from Foot's loyal colleagues. Denis Healey made himself especially available in April when there was a distinct possibility that he might quickly replace Foot. The truth of the matter appeared in a small story by the *Guardian*'s labour editor, Keith Harper, four days after Foot resigned:

> Michael Foot would have been prepared to make a dignified exit as leader of the Labour Party if there had been an October election.

> The opportunity never presented itself because Mrs Thatcher called a June election, but approaches were made to Mr Foot by

senior trade union leaders and soundings were taken in the
parliamentary Labour party before the local elections in May.
Symbiosis is a boring word but it does precisely describe the relationship between the press and politicians in this and many other political
stories. The newspapers were more than happy to publish rumours of
Foot's imminent departure while their sources hoped that the publicity
might prod him into resignation. As long as the doubters remained
anonymous Foot was safe in dismissing the stories as fabrication.

While Foot sounded off in Westminster about press smears, there
was a much better case to be made a little way down the Thames at
Bermondsey, where Peter Tatchell stood as the Labour candidate.
Foot himself had contributed much to Tatchell's notoriety by announcing from the front bench that he would do everything in his power to
prevent Tatchell standing as an official candidate. Fleet Street took the
cue and turned its attention to the obscure social worker whose
scribblings in left-wing periodicals had caused the Leader of Her
Majesty's Opposition to tremble. In him the press found a rather
unexciting, charmless individual who in many ways typified the dreary
ranks of the activist left. In no time at all Tatchell replaced Tony Benn
as bogeyman *par excellence*, a position he was to occupy until the polling
day in Bermondsey.

At first the press seemed fascinated by the candidate's dress. The
Daily Express saw him as a 'rather exotic canary who sings some odd
songs' while the *Daily Telegraph* indicated its distaste at the appearance
of this new candidate by remarking, 'Mr Tatchell, who has the habit of
drawing himself erect periodically as he talks and fingering the wide
leather belt atop trendy cord jeans and two-tone beige laced shoes,
shows considerable irritation at personal questions.'

These personal questions were most firmly put by the *Sun*
newspaper, which found Tatchell's support of gay rights, or rather his
homosexuality, the most significant part of his political life. Under the
headline, RED PETE WENT TO GAY OLYMPICS, Phil Dampier
wrote:

> Left-wing Labour candidate Peter Tatchell has upset his tough
> dockland supporters, who say he has been to the gay olympics.

They claim that the thirty year-old bachelor spent two weeks in the company of homosexuals at the bizarre sports event.

Dampier went on to quote Phil Corr, chairman of the local Young Socialists, who it seems relied upon Dampier for the information:

'Going to these olympics is the last straw. He is not doing the image of the party any good at all. He should be spending his time in Bermondsey looking after problems here, not swanning about at the gay olympics.

'What's more, as a socialist I just don't know how he can afford it.'

Mr Corr added:

'He only left Australia because he was called up into the army in the early seventies and didn't want to fight in Vietnam.

'Before that he was a marathon runner in, would you believe it, Queensland.'

This, published in September 1982, amounted to the declaration of terms on which the popular press would fight Tatchell when Bob Mellish eventually decided to stand down. Let us consider its construction carefully. In the first two paragraphs the 'tough dockland supporters' 'say' and 'claim' that Tatchell went to the gay olympics. This was untrue. The *Sun* provided the information and it is doubtful whether any of them were 'upset' about the supposed attendance until they read it in the paper. By the time we reach Phil Corr's quotes the attendance is an established fact, although absolutely nothing in the way of proof is offered. Mr Corr's quotes in the story are remarkable, encompassing all the areas in which the popular press sought to discredit Tatchell, no mean feat for a member of Mr Tatchell's own party.

Tatchell talks at length about the investigation which preceded this story in his book *The Battle For Bermondsey* (Heretic Books, 1983), which is far from entertaining but is nevertheless convincing in parts:

I was doorstepped by *Sun* reporters. At one point three of them waited outside my workplace for five hours in unseasonable cold and pouring rain to question me about an alleged visit to the gay olympics in San Francisco. I told them I knew nothing about the event before I went on holiday and did not attend it. Despite my denials, they kept non-stop pressure on me for the three days and nights to force me to confess. In the end I am sure they knew the story was fiction. But they were determined to use the coincidence of my San Francisco holiday anyway. They admitted as much when, in reply to my denial and warning about possible legal action, one of the *Sun* reporters actually said to me, 'Sue us. So what? What do we care? What's a few thousand pounds to us? This is a good story and we are going to use it.'

Not wishing to be left behind, the *Sun*'s sister paper, the *News of the World*, pushed a minor story about a move on homosexual rights at the forthcoming Labour Party Conference, which was used prominently with the headline GAY ROW ROCKS LABOUR – FREEDOM PLAN WAS BUTCHERED, SAY THE LEFTIES. This was accompanied by a retouched photograph of Tatchell which made him look as if he used eyeliner and lipstick. That week the *Daily Mail*, having spent absurd amounts of time and money in sending reporters to Australia to investigate the candidate's background, ran a centre-page spread, WHAT MAKES TATCHELL TICK, a less obvious but no less potent fiction. The paper traced a young windowdresser name Robert Kroening, with whom Peter Tatchell had once shared a house in Australia. Kroening was quoted as saying, 'Peter did most of the cooking and cleaning and I was the major breadwinner.'

When you examine the coverage that Tatchell received during that autumn of 1982 it is clear that the tabloid press was determined to keep Tatchell's undesirability in the public consciousness. The harassment he suffered was considerable. Reporters followed him everywhere, posed as council officials in the hope of eliciting complaints from his neighbours on the Rockingham estate about 'all-night homosexual parties', sifted through his rubbish in the hope of finding some damning evidence and let it be known in Bermondsey that a reward of £3,000 was on offer for anyone who could provide a good story about him. They even, apparently, pretended he had been seriously hurt in an accident in order to get access to a relative's home in Australia.

The effect, naturally enough, was to create a considerable local animus against Tatchell, so that by the time the election was under way the candidate received regular death threats and had to ask for police protection.

While the tabloids derived a certain enjoyment from the shameful bullying of a legitimate parliamentary candidate, this was not their principal motive. Since his espousal of 'extra-parliamentary action' the press had been resolved to link him with the Militant Tendency, a left-wing organisation which has subsequently been expelled from the Labour party. The simple fact of the matter was that Tatchell, whose policies were on the whole rather humdrum, unimaginative and rigidly based on the edicts of the Labour party, was not a member. True, the Militant Tendency were active in his constituency, but he had fallen out with its members on a number of occasions. The *Daily Star*, although well acquainted with this fact, neatly dodged it by simply describing his militant tendencies (using the lower case), while the *Daily Mail* constructed an entirely spurious Exclusive which claimed to have substantiated 'Militant's grip on the candidate' but did nothing of the sort. Whatever the political complexion of a publication, Tatchell seemed bound to emerge as the victim. Even when the Socialist Society, much further to the left than Tatchell, reprinted an article by him it was edited so that Tatchell appeared to be repeating a call for extra-parliamentary action.

What did the serious papers do during this time? The *Guardian* behaved impeccably and frequently made the point that Tatchell was very different from his image in the press. The *Daily Telegraph*, although never disguising its dislike of the candidate, carried fairly his accusations about press harassment and threats to his life. The *Times* ran an article by young Conservative MP Matthew Parriss, who deplored his treatment and vaguely wondered what was so threatening about him. However, the composition of the paper's front page on Polling Day left much to be desired. A photograph of Tatchell and Roy Hattersley, both looking unusually miserable, was surmounted by a highly flattering and jolly picture of the Liberal leader David Steel and his candidate Simon Hughes, the eventual victor. Beneath, Philip Webster wrote a rather bland story devoted to the imminent Alliance victory, mentioning the results of an opinion poll in that day's *Sun* which had been compiled from the reactions of six hundred telephone calls, a notoriously unreliable method of gaining opinion.

After the publicity of the preceding fifteen months it was inconceivable that Peter Tatchell would win. The *Sun* displayed its evident pleasure in an entire page headed THE SUN SPEAKS ITS MIND – always a regrettable course of action but never more so than on this occasion. Beneath another headline, THE TRUTH HURTS the nameless author wrote:

> Like the famous horizontal heavyweight, Peter Tatchell casts round for excuses and villains to explain away the disaster of Bermondsey.
>
> HE WHINES that he was the victim of a campaign of smears and lies.
>
> HE WHIMPERS that the by-election will be remembered as a black moment for journalism.
>
> Neil Kinnock, who should know better, accused the *Sun* of being chief author of Mr Tatchell's downfall.
>
> Rubbish, Mr Kinnock, no newspaper has that much power and influence. Judgments like that are an insult to the people of Bermondsey. It suggests they are gullible dupes without minds of their own.
>
> Peter Tatchell was a victim alright. A victim of truth.

When the *Sun* talks of truth one should be doubly suspicious.

By contrast the reporting of the General Election campaign was a lot less aggressive, possibly because journalists' attention was not concentrated on one constituency just a few minutes' car ride from Fleet Street. Nevertheless, the national press was far from innocent, as these two examples from the *Daily Mail* and *Daily Express* will show.

The first, from the *Daily Mail*, was such an obvious attempt to discredit the Labour party that *Private Eye* printed a mock-up of its front page, with the preposterous headline AIDS THREAT TO LABOUR VOTERS, which read as follows: 'The mystery killer disease AIDS may be related to voting labour in the General Election says a shock report made up by the *Daily Mail*.'

This was supported by the contributions of Mr Lunchtime O'Booze

(MAGGIE SAVES CHILD) and Mr Jeff Goebbels (FOOT LASHES OAP WITH STICK). There was a lot of truth in the attack. Two weeks before, at the start of the election campaign, Sir David English's paper led on a story by the motoring correspondent, Michael Kemp, who revealed that no less than 35,000 jobs would be lost to British industry if the Labour party won the election. He wrote:

> The Japanese car giant Nissan is to scrap plans for a £500 million British plant if Labour wins the election. Up to 35,000 new jobs are at stake in areas of high unemployment which are Labour strongholds.
>
> It is Labour's commitment to pull Britain out of the Common Market that is scaring Nissan.

A Nissan official was later quoted as saying, 'If Labour wins the election it is impossible to see that Nissan leaders in Japan can base a Common Market plant in Britain. They will have to site it elsewhere in the EEC.'

Mr Kemp must have pleased his superiors. It was a dream of a story which exploded both the Labour party's EEC policy and its promise to create jobs. Dream was certainly the word applied to Mr Kemp's efforts by the General Secretary of the Labour party, Jim Mortimer. He wrote to the paper, 'It seems that the *Daily Mail* fabricated a story for the purposes of persuading readers not to vote Labour.' Lord Marsh, an official consultant to the Nissan company, expressed much the same doubts, while Brian Groves, Nissan's marketing manager in Tokyo and, interestingly, Kemp's predecessor at the *Daily Mail*, said, 'We have nothing to do with it. If you ask me it came out of his head.'

Having established the potential loss of the Nissan car factory Kemp, together with a political reporter, Robin Oakley, moved on the next day to increase anxieties on this front by showing the effects a withdrawal would have on the British motor industry. At the tail of the story they carried a most illuminating quote from Nissan, which referred to the previous day's coverage: 'We think that if the Labour Party got to power it would not substantially affect our proposals. It is difficult to see Britain pulling out of the Common Market.'

Contrast with this the complete certainty of the first sentence of the original story. It is a statement of fact which one assumed Mr Kemp would have no difficulty in supporting. The *Daily Telegraph* and *Observer* ridiculed the report, so it was interesting to hear what Kemp had to say when the Press Council, hastily convened at the behest of the Labour party, started to look into the matter. He could not reveal the name of the well-informed source who, it seems, had given Kemp good stories before. The only supporting evidence that he could provide was a barely legible shorthand note (done with his left hand since his right had been injured).

The Council, although accepting Kemp as an honest witness, were unimpressed, particularly at the lack of prominence given to the denial which so completely destroyed his first story. It also criticised the *Daily Mail* for misleading readers by running an insufficiently qualified story. A question the council failed to ask was why Kemp had not approached the company formally before using the information from his source. Was it, perhaps, the knowledge that he might receive an outright denial?

In this case the Council acted with commendable speed, thus correcting the story before the election campaign was over. The same was unfortunately not true of its investigation into an article in the *Daily Express* headlined SPOT THE TROTS and written by John Warden, an experienced political correspondent who seems to have been misled by one of the horde of psephologists that pop up during election time. Douglas Eden was employed by the paper to compile a table showing the political interests and associations of seventy Labour candidates, among whom were Neil Kinnock, Dennis Skinner and Robert Hughes, the left-wing member for Aberdeen North. The real point of this chart was to demonstrate that many of these candidates were involved with groups or organisations which were considerably to the left of the Labour party and that they were therefore 'the cold, doctrinaire advocates of the all-powerful one-party state.' In the section devoted to Hughes, an amiable, golf-playing Tribunite, they attributed to him an affiliation with the Soviet Friendship Society and Friends of Afghanistan. As conclusive proof of his sinister tendencies the paper cited his contributions to the *Morning Star* and *Marxism Today*.

This came as something of a surprise to Hughes since he was not associated with either organisation and in fact had never heard of them.

He rang the *Express* to put this view in, one understands, forcible terms and mentioned that as well as writing for the *Morning Star* and *Marxism Today* he worked for other papers including the *Aberdeen Press and Journal*, hardly a mouthpiece of the anti-constitutionalist left.

After being contacted by Hughes's lawyers, the *Express* went into the classic newspaper stall and produced two more 'front' organisations that Hughes had been involved in. Hughes admitted that he had, but demonstrated that they were perfectly respectable and did not confirm him as an 'advocate of the all-powerful one-party state'.

Nine months later the *Express* appeared before the Council and admitted that it had accepted Eden's table in 'good faith' and that there had been no checking of its contents and allegations. The council found that the references to Hughes constituted a politically malicious and unjustified slur which should have been withdrawn. It also criticised the newspaper for failing to substantiate or withdraw the allegations about most of the seventy candidates it named.

Crude and unsophisticated though this may all be, there is no doubt that persistent distortion of political issues in favour of the Conservative party has a very real effect on the outcome of elections. On the one occasion when the BBC *Panorama* programme pointed out the infiltration of the party by racists from the lunatic right, the press, particularly the *Daily Mail*, did everything to discredit the evidence. Coming from the persecutors of Peter Tatchell the howls of sanctimonious rage somehow lacked conviction.

CHAPTER 5

'Yes, Minister . . . '

A day in the working life of a parliamentary lobby correspondent reads rather like a passage from Lewis Carroll. He will attend regular meetings that never take place in a room that does not exist and will put questions that are not questions to a minister or civil servant who is not there. Between these briefings, as they are known, he may make a number of telephone calls which are not made and then lunch with a close political contact whom he has never met. If there is time, he may spend an agreeable half hour or so loitering in the House of Commons Lobby, an area outside the Chamber where he is permitted by the Serjeant-at-Arms to engage Members of Parliament in conversation. Alternatively he may visit Annie's Bar, where MP's and journalists are allowed to get drunk together at any time of the day or night. Again, these exchanges never take place. At the end of the day or week, depending on whether he toils for a daily or Sunday newspaper, he will find some quiet spot in the Palace of Westminster to compose an informed piece on the mood, personalities and issues of the moment. The reader's only clue that he has not lain in a stupor all these hours and made up the lot when pressed by his deadline is the frequency with which lobby articles are punctuated by such phrases as 'informed government sources', 'usually reliable sources' and 'sources close to the Prime Minister'. These and their many ingenious variations indicate that the author is fresh from one of the collective briefings of the hundred or so lobby correspondents or has received some more personal guidance from an individual contact.

The innocent may wonder why this body of journalists go to such lengths to conceal who they have been talking to. After all, once one is familiar with the codes, it is fairly obvious that a 'source close to the Prime Minister' is the bluff and hot-tempered Bernard Ingham, her Press Secretary since 1979, who regularly presides over the daily briefing sessions. Why not come out with it? The answer, as every journalist appreciates, is that it is an essential condition of Lobby membership that the confidentiality of a source is preserved. However clear it may be that some minister or Mr Ingham has been communicating to the nation in this curiously anonymous fashion it will never be admitted by them or by the journalists they have talked to. Often the source of story is not at all obvious, particularly when it is concerned with politics more than policies, which is precisely why the elected have increasingly come to rely on the confidential procedure in the last hundred years.

There are many grounds for a reasoned criticism of lobby journalism, the very operation of which is based on deception. Recently much has been made of the discrepancy between a minister offering guidance on matters of state, while at the same time seeing to it that leaks from the departments are detected and followed by swift prosecution. During the weeks preceding the budgets of 1983 and 1984, it was apparent that certain newspapers had been given a strong steer on the contents of Sir Geoffrey Howe's and Nigel Lawson's speeches. Such indiscretion would have been unthinkable in the past, and in fact Hugh Dalton resigned as Chancellor of the Exchequer after letting slip a minor detail half an hour before the budget of 1947. Chancellor Lawson would seem to uphold this principle of absolute secrecy. He was so incensed with the *Guardian*'s accurate predictions two weeks before he rose to make his tax-reforming speech this year (1984) that he ordered an immediate police enquiry to find the source of the leak. Many members of the Lobby must have been surprised at this, since it was common, though not publishable, knowledge that Lawson himself had inspired similarly accurate predictions.

Thus one leak is acceptable guidance, while the other is a criminal breach of secrecy. The same applies to Michael Heseltine's recent announcement on the expansion of the Territorial Army. The story was leaked to the *Sunday Telegraph* before the Secretary of State had told Parliament, which prompted Merlyn Rees, a former minister who is aware of the efficacy of tactical leaking, to point out that Heseltine had just taken Sarah Tisdall to court for delivering to the *Guardian* his plans for handling the press on the arrival of American cruise missiles. Was there not some inconsistency in this? Mr Heseltine hummed and hahed and said that in this instance he could not make the distinction between a leak and a brief. I shall make it for him now. A leak is unintentional disclosure and usually causes embarrassment to a Minister or government, while a brief or 'guidance' is designed to benefit the establishment in some way. This then amounts to the most pressing argument against the Lobby system, for it is clearly as morally indefensible as it is illogical to prosecute leakers while encouraging official leaks.

People who argue for the lobby, and this is most fervently done by its membership, reply that the British way of government is by nature closed and secret. When you consider the benefits that accrue from the privileged access granted to a few trusted representatives of the press, the above inconsistency may be overlooked. The restrictions on the attribution are regrettable, but at least there is a reasonable flow of accurate information from the government, through the lobby, to the governed.

The lie to this argument is given by the simple fact that government spokesmen will always consider some pieces of information more suitable for release than others. Thus lobby journalists are presented with a selection of the government's activities and so the contents of their newspapers are managed. This hallowed access, this privileged penetration of the secret world, by no means guarantees that journalists will be given a complete and accurate picture of the life and decisions of a government. This cannot have escaped the notice of the many intelligent souls who have entered their names on the Serjeant-of-Arms's list (the official recognition of lobby membership) and set about finding out what our elected representatives are up to. Their conspicuous failure to do so may only be explained by the fact that they become too close to their subjects and, in the enjoyment of this intimacy, lose sight of their duties to truth and disclosure. In his last column for the *Sunday Times*, Hugo Young put it like this: 'For unprejudiced inquiry based on facts, they substitute a political test. In this they emulate politicians and play their game.'

There is sound enough support for this argument in the confidential parliamentary lobby rule-book which was commendably made public by the sociologist Jeremy Tunstall in his book *The Westminster Lobby Correspondents* (RKP, 1970):

Individual Lobbying:

It is the lobby correspondent's primary duty to protect his informants and care must be taken not to reveal anything that could lead to their identification . . . Sometimes it may be right to protect your informant to the extent of not using the story at all. This has often been done in the past and it forms one of the foundations of the good and confidential relationship between the lobby and members of all parties. You should do nothing to prejudice the communal life of the lobby or its good relations with the two houses and the authorities.

Collective Lobbying:

It has become common practice for ministers and others to meet the lobby collectively to give information and answer questions. Members of the lobby are under an obligation to keep secret the fact that such meetings are held, and to avoid revealing the sources of their information.

Do not talk about lobby meetings before or after they are held, especially in the presence of those not entitled to attend them. If outsiders appear to know something of the arrangements made by the lobby do not confirm their conjectures or assume that as they appear to know so much, they may safely be told the rest.

The lobby's machinery cannot operate effectively unless the courtesy and cooperation shown by ministers and officials are reciprocated.

General Hints:

Do not see anything in the Members' lobby or in any of the

private rooms or corridors of the Palace of Westminster. You are a guest of Parliament and it has always been the rule that incidents, pleasant and otherwise, should be treated as private if they happen in those parts of the building to which lobby correspondents have access because their names are on the lobby list.

Do not run after a minister or member. It is nearly always possible to place yourself in a position to avoid this. ·

The lobby activities of any colleague should not be the subject of published comment.

NEVER in ANY circumstances make use of anything accidentally overheard in any part of the Palace of Westminster.

So the watchwords are caution and discretion. There is also in these extracts a surprising tone of deference, servility even. In most areas of journalistic endeavour, reporters are, if anything, thought to be rather too self-important, but in Parliament it would appear that they are encouraged to adopt the demeanour of footmen whose livelihoods depend on toeing the line and never questioning the orders of their political masters. The self-deprecation exhorted in every line of the little leatherbound rule-book is hardly the most sensible attitude with which to approach politicians, who can at the best of times be slippery and unscrupulous fellows.

The point of the present exercise is to demonstrate the sheer quantity of inaccuracy both intentional and unintentional that appears in the national press over a particular twelve-month period. The lobby has been responsible for a certain amount, though it is fair to say that these inaccuracies are more often than not due to the trust that newspapers place in government sources. Ian Aitken, the *Guardian*'s experienced lobby man, believes that the political establishment may mislead the Lobby but not badly. He wrote:

> The simple truth is that, just as unofficial leaks are sometimes wrong, official guidance occasionally misdirects its recipients. This need not involve telling outright whoppers – an activity which is a great deal less common than the adherents of the conspiracy theory of history like to think.

Mr Aitken need only cast his mind back to the lobby briefings during the Falklands campaign to realise the error of his words. The Ministry of Defence persistently misled the lobby and other journalists with a view eventually to misleading the Argentinians over their plans for retaking the Islands. Whatever the rights and wrongs of this, it occurred and Sir Frank Cooper, the then Permanent Under-Secretary at the Ministry of Defence, has admitted that such behaviour is in his view perfectly acceptable in wartime. Interestingly, when the Commons Committee investigated the media's many complaints about the government's public relations during the spring and summer of 1982, the lobby refused to hand over tapes that proved that a number of outright whoppers had fallen from the lips of various government spokesmen (a good indication that the lobby prizes its own good relations with the government above the interests of truth and disclosure).

Another example: let us consider Mrs Thatcher's trip to the Falklands in January 1983. As far back as August 1982 it had been suggested that the Prime Minister was to attend the 150th anniversary of the expulsion of the Argentinians from the islands on January 3, 1833. The *Daily Telegraph* reported on August 10: 'The Prime Minister appears likely to visit the Falkland Islands towards the end of the year or early next year. A visit before then is not regarded as practicable.'

Tim Jones of the *Times* confirmed Downing Street's plans by reporting on August 25 that Mrs Thatcher had sent a letter to Graham Bond, the editor of *Penguin News*, the Falklands newspaper, expressing her fervent desire to mark the anniversary by a visit. The same day, however, the official disinformation service was cranked into life. The *Daily Telegraph* carried this brief announcement: 'There are no plans for the Prime Minister to visit the Falklands, a Downing Street spokesman said last night.'

Throughout the autumn of that year reports appeared alternately confirming and dismissing the idea that she would make the twelve-thousand-mile trip. In the first few days of 1983, Hugh O'Shaughnessy of the *Observer* made some inquiries at Number Ten and the Ministry of Defence, who would be responsible for arranging the visit. He was told quite categorically that Mrs Thatcher would not be going to the

Falklands. The story was used prominently in the next issue of the *Observer*, which must have pleased Downing Street. In a matter of days poor Mr O'Shaughnessy was made to look foolish when his own paper carried the news that Mrs Thatcher had, instead of spending a quiet weekend at Chequers, boarded a flight to the Islands. He was left to add the following footnote to the front-page lead, which itself made an interesting point about the value of the Prime Minister being photographed in a combat jacket among grateful islanders:

> The Prime Minister's decision to go ahead with the Falklands trip comes quickly after the earlier cancellation of her planned visit scheduled for last Monday . . . Her presence will help her weather any criticism of government neglect of the Islands in the months before the Argentine invasion in the Franks report which is expected to be published later this month.

As with the Falklands war, there may have been powerful arguments and good intentions behind the disinformation, but it is no good Aitken and his colleagues protesting that they are always told the unvarnished truth. The Lobby and, for that matter other journalists, who deal with government spokesmen are frequently lied to, and often on the instructions of the Prime Minister.

When the cabinet papers were released from official secrecy at the end of 1983, most newspapers made much of the official cover-up of Sir Winston Churchill's stroke. A.J. McIlroy demonstrated in the *Daily Telegraph* how officials, with the approval of Churchill, hid his illness from the public by doctoring medical bulletins, manipulating Fleet Street photographers and delivering outright denials to lobby journalists. Even after thirty years the *Telegraph* thought that story sufficiently interesting to devote the whole of its valuable page three to it and write a leader on the topic of suppression. One wonders why the paper and the rest of Fleet Street did not devote more space to similar activities in Downing Street in August 1983, when the press office put so much effort into misleading Fleet Street on the true nature of Mrs Thatcher's eye operation.

On Sunday July 31, Mrs Thatcher was driven from Chequers to Windsor for emergency laser treatment on her right eye. No details were given to the press until the following day, when Downing Street issued a statement to the effect that she had scratched her retina by rubbing a bit of grit into it at a Buckingham Palace garden party the previous week. As Michael Cockerell, Peter Hennessy and David Walker point out in their book *Sources Close To The Prime Minister*, this was medical nonsense. The retina is at the back of the eye and it would be impossible to inflict such an injury by the mere action of rubbing. Nevertheless, the national press dutifully reported the Number Ten version – there was no hint given that Mrs Thatcher had undergone laser surgery. On Tuesday August 2, word leaked out that the retina might have been more seriously damaged. The *Daily Telegraph* reported:

> Dr John Henderson, her family practitioner, advised her to rest yesterday and particularly cut down on paperwork in the hope that the irritation would heal itself. But if her condition is not improved by tomorrow when an eye surgeon is to call she may have to go into hospital for laser surgery. Official sources were taking a relaxed view of the disorder.

The same was true of the press. On Wednesday August 3, the following headlines appeared: THATCHER DOCTOR HOPEFUL (*Daily Telegraph*); PM MAY AVOID EYE SURGERY (*Guardian*) and DOCTOR OPTIMISTIC ABOUT MRS THATCHER'S EYE (*The Times*). All quoted Dr Henderson as saying she was 'unfussed by it all and is carrying on with a little dictation and that sort of thing'. The impression given, therefore, was that there was absolutely no call for alarm. The Prime Minister was carrying on with a little work, Number Ten was 'relaxed' and Mrs Thatcher's deputy, Viscount Whitelaw, had not been recalled from his holiday in Scotland.

By Thursday, however, Downing Street admitted that she had not only received laser treatment on the previous Sunday, but that this had unexpectedly failed. Late that night the press office announced that another operation had taken place under general anaesthetic. The *Guardian*'s Colin Brown wrote:

> There was some surprise when it was learned that Mrs Thatcher had already undergone laser treatment at the weekend. It was

thought the option remained open and last night Downing Street strongly denied that they had covered up the extent of Mrs Thatcher's eye problem. They said that they were acting in accordance with the Prime Minister's wishes.

The rest of the press was similarly mild in its remarks. The *Daily Mail*, low down in its front page lead, simply said, 'The clear implication of Whitehall guidance on Monday was that no question of an operation was likely to arise until yesterday (Wednesday).'

Let us just review the stages of this deception: i) Her original operation, though a matter of legitimate concern for the press, was suppressed; ii) When Downing Street admitted that she had some eye trouble they described it wrongly and underplayed it; iii) By Wednesday the press office gave the distinct impression that she was on the mend, when, in fact, her condition had deteriorated; iv) Although the Prime Minister was incapacitated for over a week, Lord Whitelaw was not summoned to London to stand in for her. This, too, one imagines to have been part of the subterfuge.

What is so extraordinary about this episode is that Fleet Street, when noting the correct version of the facts, only referred in passing to this suppression. There seems to be an acceptance that this sort of lying is part of the cat-and-mouse game between the Fourth Estate and the political establishment. The fact that the Prime Minister herself commissioned the deception seems to have made it no more reprehensible. True, her operation was not a spectacularly important issue, but the behaviour of her staff does raise one or two serious questions about the ethics current in the Number Ten press office. If it behaves in this way on such a minor story, how can the press possibly trust its guidance on major issues?

The story, I think, is illustrative of the contempt in which the political establishment, by which I mean Whitehall, the Cabinet, Party Managers in the Commons and Downing Street, hold the press. Journalists are there to convey the establishment's version of the facts to the nation. This may be resisted in some parts of the Lobby, but generally the practice of accepting the word of one source without checking it with another means that government spokesmen and

Ministers get away with a lot of 'misdirection' and even 'outright whoppers'. Of course the attitude of governments towards Fleet Street is never entirely dismissive or hostile and both parties recognise the value of patronage which includes knighthoods to loyal editors (Sir John Junor, Sir David English and Sir Larry Lamb), exclusive stories to favoured Lobby correspondents, interviews to friendly newspapers and even preferential treatment in the allocation of rooms in the Leader's hotel at annual party conferences. While these currently apply to the Conservative party, it is as well to mention that the Labour party is no less cynical in the judicious use of rewards, as the executives of the Daily Mirror Group during the Wilson and Callaghan years can testify. However solicitous and helpful government ministers and spokesmen appear to be, journalists should be sure that behind it lies a steely determination to present the government in the best possible light.

Bernard Ingham was away from Number Ten during the week of Mrs Thatcher's illness. Whether he would have handled the press with any more adroitness it is difficult to say, but doubtless he would have complied with the Prime Minister's instructions. Ingham's influence round and about Whitehall has become considerable; the following document will demonstrate both this and the prevalent arrogant view of the press. Towards the end of 1983 Mr Ingham and the Prime Minister became much exercised by the lack of enthusiasm both in the media and among government back-benchers for the Conservative party's plans for local government reform. He put together a plan for neutralising the Tory dissidents and, more important, for taking the initiative from the critics of the government proposals by a concentrated campaign in the media. Now, it is to be expected that Mr Ingham, a loyal and diligent civil servant, will do his utmost to put the government's case, but his confidential circular to five ministers, gratifyingly leaked to the local government correspondent of the *Guardian*, John Carvel, carries one or two disturbing phrases which might have caused journalists to wonder how much they were being used by the administration. The public relations action that he proposed included lobby briefings for editors, specialist correspondents and leader writers, the use of newspaper correspondence columns to put the government's point of view and making available senior politicians for interviews and guest columns. (Incidentally, an extremely dull piece by the Secretary of State for the Environment, Patrick Jenkin, was being hawked about Fleet Street at the time. The *Sunday Times* for one turned it down, but the *Sunday Express* editor, Sir John Junor, obligingly carried it.) What should make journalists sit up and think is the advice that, 'REMEDIAL ACTION SHOULD BE TAKEN AGAINST TROUBLESOME JOURNALS, WHETHER NATIONAL, PROVINCIAL OR SPECIAL-IST'. What he intended by this we shall never know because he was so enraged by the publication of the memorandum that he refused to enlarge on the subject. However, we may be certain that this remedial action would involve the nobbling of certain journalists and possibly the withdrawal of government favours.

The point one should emphasise here is that the lobby is regarded by politicians of whatever party as a legitimate instrument of propaganda. On some occasions it will serve the government's interest to be candid and on others selective or deliberately deceitful. Take the speculation over the date of the last general election. It suited the Conservative party that the Opposition should think that Mrs Thatcher would not go to the country until the autumn and possibly after. The Labour party, as we have seen, was in the middle of one of its habitual crises at the beginning of 1983. Most of the senior figures were themselves using the lobby to cast doubt on Michael Foot's ability to lead the party in a general election. If the Tories could persuade them that there was time enough to drop Foot and start the cumbersome procedures for electing a new leader and open up all the wounds that that would entail, so much the better. Thus it was no coincidence that in January the *Standard* carried the prominent assertion that there would be no June election. With the benefit of hindsight, it is clear that the Conservatives were always going to opt for June. The memory of the Falklands campaign was still fresh, inflation was down and steady and the party and its leader had an unprecedented lead in the polls. Doubtless the *Standard* believed the story to be true, but an understanding of the government's desire to fog the issue should have made the newspaper suspicious.

The final example of the abuse of the Lobby system is most apt, bêcause it demonstrates how an individual politician may use the terms of confidentiality to his own advantage, and because it concerns Cecil Parkinson as the master of the planted rumour and the judicious leak. Parkinson's period of almost unassailable influence in the Thatcher administration came to an end in the second week of October 1983 when it was disclosed that he had had an affair with his secretary Sara Keays and that she was expecting his child. Fleet Street had been uncharacteristically reluctant to investigate the rumours circulating at the top of the Conservative party. The *Daily Mirror* went so far as to confirm them but, owing to Mike Molloy's distaste for such revelation, failed to publish. In the event *Private Eye* forced Parkinson and Keays into a public statement by referring to her condition, wrongly attributing it to the activities of a wholly innocent back-bencher. During the first week of the scandal it looked as if Parkinson, Mrs Thatcher's closest advisor, might survive. He produced a creditable performance on the BBC's *Panorama* programme which won the sympathy of the Conservative rank and file who were assembling in Blackpool for the annual party conference. It did not, however, go down very well in a small cottage in the Home Counties, where Sara Keays was confined as much by the press as by her condition. She let it be known to the *Times* that she contested much of what her former lover had said and that she would give an interview correcting certain elements of his story, not least the question of whether he had, or had not, promised to marry her during the previous summer. Early the following day Parkinson announced his resignation and returned with his wife Ann to their home in Hertfordshire.

This resumé of the Parkinson affair is necessary because it is essential to an understanding of his dealings with the *Sunday Times* in the succeeding twenty-four hours. After the unceasing public discussion of his infidelity, the ex-minister showed no particular inclination to respond in detail to Miss Keays's allegations. However, the new editor of the *Sunday Times*, Andrew Neil, decided to chance his luck by sending a hand-delivered letter to Parkinson's home, suggesting that he put his side of the story in the *Sunday Times*. A reply did not come until well after midday on Saturday, by which time the political staff and a

news reporter had put together a story consisting mainly of unattribut-
able and vaguely sympathetic quotes from the cabinet – colleagues.
Parkinson telephoned Neil and gave an extensive interview on lobby
terms and on the express condition that the paper would disguise the
contribution. This might have gone undetected had not a number of
senior executives and the proprietor of the paper, Rupert Murdoch,
been alerted to the conversation (Mr Murdoch was apparently so taken
by the story that he started writing the bills which would plaster the
news stands the next day). The *Sunday Times* news desk was informed
that it could shortly expect an exclusive interview with Parkinson and
that it should prepare a fresh front page. The piece, penned by Neil and
including a little information from the first story, duly arrived. It was
printed as an Exclusive, and headlined THE CASE FOR PARKINSON
– EX-MINISTER FRIENDS SPEAK OUT:

> In an atmosphere of increasing bitterness, Cecil Parkinson's
> friends yesterday rounded on Miss Keays and her family, accus-
> ing her of a wilful campaign to destroy the career of her former
> lover. They also made it clear that they did not accept significant
> details of her version of the affair and delivered point-by-point
> refutations of her statement to the *Times* last week.
> One government minister who did not wish to be named said, 'I
> am always willing to think the best of anyone, but no one can
> describe her as a sweet young woman.'
> Parkinson's friends specifically rejected the claim, made in
> Sara Keays's statement to the *Times* that their baby was conceived
> in 'a long-standing loving relationship'. They claim that there had
> been a 'clear break' in the relationship lasting several years and
> that he had only seen her 'two or three times' this year.
> A government minister said of Parkinson last night, 'It's
> remarkable that he kept going throughout the election campaign
> with that woman ringing him up twice a day and asking him about
> the divorce. We should be grateful that he kept the flag flying.
> Strangely enough it was Sara Keays who was getting all the hate
> mail.'
> Parkinson's friends do not excuse his behaviour in resuming

the affair though they say he was amazed when she told him she was pregnant. His political allies are particularly furious about Keays's complaint that he refused to keep the Prime Minister fully informed.

Last night, when Parkinson was told by the *Sunday Times* about his friends rallying to his defence, he said, 'I have no further comment to make. Any friend who has the interests of me and my family at heart should refrain from any further comment. They are doing me no favour.'

But they clearly believe otherwise. What they said yesterday was uncompromising and unanimous.

All of the Parkinson allies who spoke to the *Sunday Times* suspect that the Keays camp thought that the statement would be enough alone to break Parkinson. They say there was a mounting anger when Parkinson survived the *Panorama* interview.

Keays referred in the *Times* to the Panorama interview as breach of the agreement that both sides should say no more about the affair. Parkinson's friends say that he spoke only in the most general terms and entirely about the effect of the affair in his role as a cabinet minister.

Parkinson's friends are aware that, by giving their version of events, they could provoke Keays into another damaging attack. But they are anxious to set the record straight nevertheless. Nobody close to either Parkinson or Keays expects the two to become lovers or even friends for a third time.

When this appeared there was, to put it mildly, a good deal of unease in the *Sunday Times* newsroom. Reporters pointed out that the piece was almost entirely based on quotations and information attributed to supporters of the ex-minister. The truth, of course, was that these, almost without exception, were supplied by Parkinson himself. The only paragraph ascribed to him was the quotation asking his friends to desist from further comment, a device insisted upon by Parkinson to throw the scent. In fact the source was not especially well disguised. With a close reading it is easy to see that much of the information could only have come from Parkinson. There was other criticism too. Here was a front-page news story which had dropped any pretence of independence; the bias was even declared in the headline.

The final edition of the paper carried some minor changes to the story which principally concerned the sequence between May and June when Sara Keays became pregnant. These were provided by other sources and confirmed by Parkinson. However, the general tone remained the same.

One *Sunday Times* journalist, who was, to use a lobby phrase, close to the editor of the *Sunday Times*, summed up the objections to the story in this way: 'The Lobby system is invidious enough anyway but when someone like Parkinson uses it to settle some score with a girlfriend whom he had got pregnant that is a real abuse. The whole final edition story was based on Parkinson's phone call and that was not good enough. I would say that it was an extremely injudicious story. We could have done one on how Parkinson was trying to manipulate the press. The *Sunday Times* was not the only paper phoned on that Saturday.'

The convenience of the Lobby system for journalists as well as politicians is obvious. It is difficult to underestimate the attraction of accepting its restrictions in order to fill column inches with the minimum of effort, as I know myself. However dubious his motives, it is easy to accept a politician's word when one is pressed for time and material. The most disturbing aspect of the system is the way in which it has spread to other groups of specialist journalists. Education, Defence, Diplomatic, Industrial and Economic correspondents all conspire to conceal their sources in branches of the executive. Even Scotland Yard has adopted a form of the Lobby System whereby a group of trusted journalists is fed with information on a non-attributable basis. In pursuit of an easy life journalists have progressively relegated themselves to the status of mere instruments of government propaganda.

CHAPTER 6

Punk Rockers, Several Women and
Self-Confessed Marxists

Newspapers, it is popularly understood, gather and report news. This is to ignore their function as a target for any group or individual with a cause to publicise, whether commercial, political or personal.

I once met an American publisher who was in Britain to help publicise a new and, he hoped, controversial biography of the former Secretary of State Henry Kissinger. He had few doubts about the worth of his trip since he thought the British press was among the most susceptible to publicity campaigns in the world. He said that this was because the average newspaper journalist here is a supine, undiscerning and passive creature who had long ago abandoned the spirit of inquiry that represented true journalistic endeavour in favour of the neatly typed publicity handout, or the generous lunch where he is fed wine and information in roughly equal proportions. American reporters, on the other hand, were not so easily manipulated since the qualities of diligence and independence were inculcated in the apprentices of the profession in his country's many excellent schools of journalism. I have my doubts about journalism as an academic discipline and such as I have seen of American newspapers has led me to think that he was not talking from a position of unassailable perfection. Still, his main point, that the British press is unusually receptive to the blandishments of the public relations industry, is true. How often is the same personality interviewed in half a dozen newspapers within the space of a few days. And how depressing it is to open all the popular newspapers for one day only to find the same ludicrous publicity gimmicks photographed and written up in all of them.

The fact is that much of the content of the national press is inspired by companies wishing to plug some product, some service or some personality and is therefore little more than covert advertising. Thus the manufacturers of women's tights will organise a 'Miss Lovely Legs' competition (almost guaranteed coverage in the popular press) and brewers will sponsor yacht races round the world, and margarine manufacturers will commission damaging surveys into the effects of eating butter, and the makers of pet foods will run competitions to find the friendliest mongrel and so forth. All are designed to promote something to someone's commercial advantage and the press in most cases is very obliging. I do not find anything particularly alarming or sinister in this; if newspapers are going to draw on the public relations industry for novel and interesting ideas it seems only fair that the publicity agents should be repaid with the tacit endorsement of their goods.

Politicians in this country were a little slow to recognise the benefits of public relations, and agents were for the most part seen to have a defensive role. However, they now appear to have got the message and not only employ advertising agencies but also use publicity gimmicks to win favourable coverage in newspapers. Thus we find Mrs Thatcher entertaining the cast of *Anyone For Dennis* at Number Ten and reading her own script with the stars of the B.B.C. TV programme *Yes, Minister*. Likewise, we are presented with the spectacle of Neil Kinnock performing an engaging duo with a pop singer. None of these spontaneous displays of affection for well-known showpeople would have taken place if newspapers and television did not exhibit such a crass willingness to be used.

By any definition you care to take none of these stunts are really news. This is not to say that news *must* be spontaneous and unprompted, since a goodly proportion of 'the news' is the result of groups or individuals drawing attention to their cause and seeking to infiltrate their case into the public awareness. Every day newspapers are assailed with the reports of the activities of groups as disparate as the Peace Movement, Action on Smoking and Health, Animal Liberation, Greenpeace, the Campaign for Real Ale and even the Hot Food Take-Away Lobby. All go about creating in public with the specific aim of getting coverage. There is, though, a rather odd inconsistency in the newspapers' attitude to these publicity stunts. They will give faithful and accurate record of a Miss Lovely Legs competition but when it comes to disarmament marches or unemployment demonstrations they seem to wake up and wonder if they are not being used rather too much.

A good example of this concerned the People's March For Jobs 1983. Two years previously the trade unions and Labour party had organised a roughly similar exercise, which in turn had been inspired by the great hunger marches of the Depression. The point, of course, was to draw attention to the plight of the young unemployed. The first march was relatively well received by the press. I covered it and there was not a great deal to write about. One or two popular newspapers had sent representatives to find out what the marchers got up to at night with a view to running 'love on the dole' stories, but for the most part journalists filed pictures and even reports about the marchers and their route through the English countryside. The 1983 version was altogether less fairly treated, possibly because there was nothing new for newspapers to say, but more probably because the march, which set off from different parts of the country a month before the General Election, did much to expose the Conservative government's record on employment. For the month of the march's progress to London the press responded unfavourably and did much to discredit its case. No newspaper did more in this cause than the *Daily Express*, which in the shape of Peter Kent exposed the marchers as being more interested in demonstrations than in gainful employment. Under the headline WORK GALORE BUT THE JOB MARCHERS JUST PASS BY he wrote the following story:

Hundreds of jobs were yesterday offered to 74 demonstrators marching on London to protest about unemployment.

But the marchers turned down every one of the openings offered by the job centre manager.

One protestor raised his arm in a clench fist salute and said, 'We are fed up with job centres and the cardboard cut-outs who work in them.'

Then walking on he said, 'I'm sorry we have not time to talk.'

The protestors, including punk rockers, several women and self-confessed Marxists, arrived in the market town of Carnforth, Lancashire, on the thirteenth day of the People's March For Jobs chanting, 'We want work . . . we want work.'

But they were jeered by housewives on street corners. One group shouted, 'Bloody Trots, there's work if you want it.'

And there was, offered by the Manpower Services Commission which forecasts that the Morecambe–Lancaster region around Carnforth will be 'a land of golden opportunity' within a year with thousands of jobs available.

And a spokesman threw out this golden opportunity to the marchers. 'There are plenty of jobs available now. It is just a question of whether there are vacancies that match the jobs you are looking for.

If you come in we'll give you a friendly, and hopefully, helpful response.'

The Lancaster–Morecambe region which has jobs available has an unemployment rate of 13.9 per cent compared with a national average of 13.5 per cent. The number of unemployed in the region is 6,610.

So the *Daily Express* had found conclusive proof of the oft-stated notion that the 'punk rockers, women and self-confessed Marxists' were simply professional demonstrators. Mr Kent himself appeared to have witnessed a member of the Manpower Services Commission stop the seventy-four demonstrators in the road and offer each and every one of them work in the land of 'golden opportunity'. Certainly Mr Kent's use of the vocative case in the quotations indicates that the job centre manager (who is nowhere named in the story) is addressing the marchers in person. The response, 'we are fed up with job centres and the cardboard cut-outs who work in them' would seem to be the typical churlish rebuttal of the left.

In fact, and there is little of it here, what really happened (as the Press Council judgment was to show) was that Kent had visited the job centre, found the number of vacancies in the area and conveyed the statistic to the marchers himself; a very different story to the encounter which is portrayed in his report. Mr Kent later, in evidence to the Press Council, explained that this, surely the most relevant part of the story, had been excluded by a *Daily Express* sub-editor. But the entire tone and construction of the piece relied on the offer being made by a job centre manager. If the phrase 'through the *Daily Express*' had been added there would have been very little point in running the story. In the light of this admission the rest of the report must be treated with the deepest suspicion, particularly the quotation from an anonymous group of housewives which expressed precisely the feelings of the *Daily Express* and presumably Mr Kent.

In the same edition of the paper, a main leader on the subject of the People's March For Jobs commented that the local job centre had offered three times as many jobs as there were marchers and that it was significant that the march was so short of people. This of course was misleading since the *Daily Express* knew, or ought to have known, that many hundreds of marchers were converging from different parts of the country. The leader is interesting for another reason. As far as I know it is common practice in Fleet Street for leader writers, whose pages generally go to press before the news pages, to be given copies of stories they are commenting on before the sub-editors have tackled them. One assumes, therefore, that the leader writer in this case was fully aware of the fact that the offer of jobs had been made through the paper and not the job centre. Why was there no mention of this?

The answer, I believe, is that the *Express* was determined to show the People's March For Jobs '83 in the worst possible light. But perhaps I malign the leader-writer; it may be that he only received a bowdlerised version of the report and thus had no knowledge of Kent's initiative. If this was the case the *Express* ought to revise its procedure for briefing the people who articulate the views of 'the Voice of Britain'.

That the People's March For Jobs actively courted publicity should of course make absolutely no difference to the way in which it is subsequently covered. The same principle applies to the Peace Movement, perhaps the most highly organised, most motivated and eloquent pressure group to occupy the media during 1983. In many ways, 1983 represented the peak of the movement's remarkable growth which began four or five years ago in the general concern over the new generation of intercontinental and, more especially, short-range nuclear missiles. At first the press seemed unable to make up its mind whether the demonstrations were a threat to the order of the western hemisphere or a commendable display of concern for the future of the planet. The early marches were reported dispassionately and it must be said that the Campaign for Nuclear Disarmament benefited from the coverage, winning more support, not to mention subscriptions and other financial help. But as the campaign was advanced by the press so it was eventually to be harmed.

During 1982 there had been growing concern in Whitehall, particularly the Ministry of Defence, about the strength of the movement. The Conservative government felt that it had failed to respond to the arguments of the Peace Movement; it had lost the propaganda war so far and would continue to do so unless it began to put its own case more forcibly. There was an urgency because it was clear that the Prime Minister would be going to the country within the next year and obvious that the nuclear issue would play a large part in a General Election. Whitehall started at the top by briefing a number of friendly editors and defence correspondents about the need for cruise missiles and also the sinister complexion of C.N.D.'s political affiliations. The reasoning was that the campaign consisted broadly of two groups of people: the well-meaning but ill-informed majority who genuinely believed that unilateral disarmament would advance the interests of peace, and the influential minority which was deemed to be working on behalf of the Warsaw Pact countries. In other words C.N.D. was made up of the dupes and friends of Moscow. There can be no objection to the government putting its case openly and fairly, but these adverbs would not seem to be the most appropriate to describe Whitehall's activities in the spring of 1983.

Two individuals were especially energetic in feeding information into the press. Winston Churchill, who occasionally attempts to wear the mantle of his grandfather in defence matters, was put in charge of the Conservative coordinating committee at Central Office, which was responsible for heightening awareness in the party and the country about the threat posed by C.N.D. and Russian forces; and Doctor Julian Lewis, the Research Director of the Coalition for Peace which, significantly, operated from 27/31 Whitehall. The precise relationship between Lewis and Churchill was never entirely clear; however, it is safe to say that Dr Lewis would agree completely with Churchill's claim that 'C.N.D. have made themselves the standard bearers of the three foreign-policy objectives of the Kremlin, it is stuffed full of communists, Marxists and socialists.' Adam Raphael, the *Observer*'s political editor, revealed their interdependence in an article, headed THE ROOTS OF A TORY SMEAR AGAINST CND, in which he proved that Churchill circulated leaflets produced by Lewis. One, entitled 'Communists, Neutralists and Defeatists', read: 'The Defeatists of the 1930s have come back to life in the 1980s – they call themselves the Campaign for Nuclear Disarmament.' Churchill was remarkably sensitive on the matter and tried at first to deny that his committee had been distributing the leaflets, but eventually admitted it and went on to issue an unbalanced statement on the political constituency of the Peace Movement. In itself the pamphlet does not appear to be particularly damaging and was likely only to confirm beliefs which were already held. However it is illustrative of the sort of things the Conservative party were up to.

Raphael's article appeared on May 8, just a month from polling day. He might, perhaps, have made a better case against the Conservative party's smear tactics had he cast a critical eye over the previous fortnight's newspapers, all of which displayed a remarkably unanimous concern for the political makeup of C.N.D. The Defence Secretary had called the tune by announcing that he was sending a letter to all Conservative candidates outlining the links between the Labour party and C.N.D., and giving some brief biographical details of the C.N.D.'s leadership. On May 4 Patrick Cosgrave, a freelance journalist who earns a modest living between Downing Street and Fleet Street, wrote a barely readable leader-page article in the *Daily Express* entitled MOSCOW LINK WITH BAN THE BOMB PROTESTORS: EXPOSED THE HARD LEFT BEHIND CND. It was little more than a list of names from the top of C.N.D., giving their former or current political affiliations. Needless to say the Moscow link was not exposed. I mention Cosgrave's effort because it bears a quite astonishing similarity to a '*Daily Mail* investigation' that appeared the same week. Tim Miles, the author, produced virtually the same list, though in a different order. I am not suggesting that Cosgrave or Miles plagiarised each other, merely that they were over-reliant on the propaganda which was dished out to Conservative candidates by Heseltine and purveyed in the scribblings of Dr Julian Lewis. There seems to be little doubt that the C.N.D. hierarchy was broadly of the left and there can be no objection to newspapers pointing this out. It is the abject way Fleet Street took its timing and information from the government and Whitehall which is so depressing.

On the whole I do not think that C.N.D. suffered unduly. During the research for this book I visited the Campaign's headquarters in London, where I was shown Monsignor Bruce Kent's 'smear file'. It was surprisingly slim and consisted mostly of reports about the dis-agreements within C.N.D. over its policy toward NATO. Interestingly, the C.N.D. press officer Alison Whyte was unable to single out many examples of wholesale fabrication. C.N.D., however, did suffer from a considerable bias, which for the most part was expressed in the emphasis of news stories, their headlines and in their language rather than in actual fiction. During 1983 there was a rather entertaining dispute over the ownership of the word 'peace'. In the same way as democracy and freedom are fought over by groups with radically differing views, both unilateralists and multilateralists felt they should have exclusive rights over peace. Broadly speaking writers and newspapers that were opposed to C.N.D. and Greenham Common used peace in inverted commas, thus planting a doubt in the reader's mind about the real intentions of the 'Peace' Movement. There was also the emergence of an interesting neologism, 'peacemongering'. Wars are, of course, usually mongered, so the word rather neatly incorporated the multilateralists' view that unilateralists were in fact little more than warmongers.

Headlines are great indicators of bias. Take the front page of the *Standard* of December 20, 1983, which read, 'CND HOLDING

HANDS WITH IRA' – POLICE ANGER AS DEMOS TAKE MEN OFF BOMB WATCH DUTY.

The implication is clear; three days after the ghastly Harrods bomb, the Peace Movement is actively supporting the I.R.A. in its Christmas bombing campaign. The headline is calculated to create animosity towards the Peace Movement, although of course the story by Bob Grahame proved that the C.N.D. supporters were merely demonstrating against the arrival of the cruise missile. The headline is supported from a quote from an anonymous police inspector: 'If another bomb goes off in central London these people can be held culpable. They are simply holding hands with the I.R.A.'

It is obvious to anyone who pauses to think that his remark, which we must accept as accurate, is nonsense. Of course C.N.D. had nothing to do with the bombing campaign. If the Police Inspector was going to make such damaging and ludicrous allegations he should have put his name to them. But more important the newspaper should never even have contemplated using the headline without some form of attribution.

Here is another headline which linked peace protestors with violence: CHAOS AT MARCH AS SEVENTEEN HELD. It appeared in Sir John Junor's *Sunday Express* the day after C.N.D. held a large rally in London which most newspapers conceded was attended by 200,000 people. I have always understood the word chaos to mean a state of utter disorder. Seventeen people held on minor charges out of a total of 200,000 is hardly worth a mention, let alone the extravagant use of the word chaos. In fact it represents a crime rate of 0.001 per cent, a figure that the most sleepy market town in Britain might envy.

Obviously the event was severely misrepresented in the headline. However Sir John, who always takes a robust attitude towards the Press Council, was not prepared to admit it. He argued that the report had been unusually balanced and that his reporters had seen the 'throwing of bottles and the many bloodied faces' which had not been used in the story. This is difficult to credit; if a *Sunday Express* reporter had seen these things there is not the slightest doubt that his editor would have expected him to use them to great effect. In this case the Press Council produced an interesting judgment which is more important than the complaint of bias in the headline. While upholding the accusation that the use of the word chaos was emotive and utterly unjustified the adjudication said, 'The newspaper was entitled to be partisan and though the report was highly selective the Press Council is satisfied that it was accurate.'

My own view, and with a little thought the Press Council might concur, is that newspapers are entitled to be partisan in their editorial pages but not in their news reports. One hopes that this was a temporary failure of judgment since if the Council concedes the notion of impartial news reporting the future looks very bleak indeed. Fortunately it seems only to have been an aberration, since the Council emphasised precisely this principle when dealing with the *Sun* which, it goes without saying, is always in the vanguard of those wishing to protect us from the Peace Movement. Under the headline CND: IS IT ALL A RUSSIAN CON TRICK? MOSCOW MAKING FOOLS OF OUR BAN THE BOMB BRIGADE the newspaper reported that nineteen members of various peace groups had visited Moscow to talk about disarmament with equivalent Soviet groups. The visit was organised by the Northern Friends of Peace Board, an offshoot of the Quaker movement which has pacifist convictions that go back to the mid-seventeenth century. The delegation also included the venerable and distinguished peace campaigner Lord Brockway and Father Owen Hardwicke, a Roman Catholic priest. The *Sun* described them thus: 'They are part of a campaign orchestrated and financed by the Soviet Union.'

While papers on the right in Fleet Street have often voiced such suspicions no reporter has actually managed to confirm them. The *Sun* provided no more evidence than anybody else, but was either sufficiently confident of its instinct or so rooted in its bias as to present the opinion as an established fact. In defence at the Press Council hearing, Henry Douglas, the *Sun*'s legal manager, who seems to spend a great deal of time at Salisbury Square explaining the idiosyncracies of the newspaper's reporting staff, said, 'The newspaper stood by its right to express its opinion, however unpalatable, on anyone who officially or unofficially took part in international affairs.' Clearly comment is allowed to range freely through the contents of the newspaper whatever the threat to factual accuracy. One should just add that in this case the *Sun* was so anxious to put over its message that it failed to get a simple fact like the month of the visit right. Happily the Press Council upheld the complaint of the Northern Friends Peace Board saying:

> This and its content might have been appropriate to trenchant editorial comment but were out of place in a news report . . . it seriously misrepresented the activities of the Northern Friends Peace Board by suggesting it was part of a campaign orchestrated and financed by the Soviet Union with the direct purpose of weakening the West. The assertion was unsubstantiated and should not have been made.

It is evidence of the Peace Movement's motivation and organisation that it has so often and so successfully complained to the Press Council. The Council has not always found in its favour, but at least it has been allowed to air its grievances far more than most groups or individuals who are abused by the press. This businesslike approach may also be seen in the way the Movement, and particularly the Greenham Common Peace Camp, went about getting publicity for themselves.

The camp started in a relatively aimless fashion in 1981 when a small group of women walked from Cardiff to the then obscure air base a little way from Newbury. For well over a year the camp went virtually ignored by the national press. There seemed to be little of a novel or newsworthy nature in their aspiration to prevent the siting of these medium range missiles. However, by the winter of 1982–3 the women had, through their endurance, proved the strength of their conviction, and they began to receive some encouraging publicity (notably in the *Observer*) which had the desired effect of drawing attention to Greenham and attracting a greater number of women protestors to the camp. Soon controversy was achieved when the women, to the obvious embarrassment of the authorities, invaded the camp. Photographs of women dancing about on the sinister tumuli under which the missiles and their transporters would eventually be housed marks the point at which the media began to take a serious interest in the camp. The women were no longer just a collection of cranks mouthing nonsense about international motherhood and the innate evil and aggression to be found in men, but rather a well-organised threat to the security of the base which had the ability to make the authorities look extremely silly and had learnt enough about the media to tip off a photographer in advance when it did so. But while there was much guile in their attraction of publicity there was much innocence in their expectation that the media would convey to the nation the self-evident rectitude of their cause. As the year passed their imaginative activities began to irritate rather than convince. The 'die-ins', the hollering, the keening, singing and dancing; the painted faces and the use of mirrors 'to reflect the evil back into the airbase' appeared to the public to be exhibitionist and meaningless, whatever the sincerity with which they were performed.

Nevertheless the fact that the Greenham Common Women were, like the People's March for Jobs '83, courting the press did not justify the considerable licence that newspaper reporters granted themselves in covering these activities. The first real damage was inflicted by the reporting of Michael Heseltine's visit to Newbury to address local Conservatives. Heseltine had been asked by the Conservative MP Michael McNair Wilson in 1982 when he was Secretary of State for Environment. Announcing that the visit would still go ahead, the *Daily Mail* observed, 'It is usual when a minister changes jobs to cancel the talk or to give the hosts an opportunity to call it off.' But Heseltine, who is as shrewd as he is publicity-conscious, did not; one suspects he realised that in this modest constituency meeting there would be ample opportunity for redressing the balance in the publicity way. The reaction of the Greenham Common Women, and perhaps of the media too, exceeded all expectations. On February 8, 1983, the national newspapers carried the following headlines: MOBBED: HESELTINE IS FLOORED (the *Sun*); PEACE CAMP WOMEN MOBBED HESELTINE (the *Daily Telegraph*); TARZAN'S WAR – HESELTINE FELLED BY WOMEN (*Daily Mirror*); JEERING PROTESTORS PUNCH MINISTER (*The Times*); FURY OF PEACE WOMEN – HESELTINE SENT CRASHING DURING NUCLEAR PROTEST (*Daily Express*); ANGRY PEACE GIRLS ROUGH UP HESELTINE (the *Sun*). In the accounts Mr Heseltine was variously 'sent crashing', 'dragged to the ground', 'punched', 'pushed', 'kicked', 'hissed at', and 'spat upon'. He could barely have hoped for a more fruitful trip down the M4. While he was shown in a rather heroic light the women's behaviour was vaguely reminiscent of a lively Saturday afternoon on the terraces of Millwall football club. The facts, though, were rather different to the way in which the dailies presented them. While there was undoubtedly confusion outside Newbury Town Hall the Minister of Defence was neither 'dragged to the ground', 'punched', 'kicked' or 'pushed'. He fell over. How do we know this? Because Mr Heseltine said so. The facts were later confirmed in a Ministry of Defence statement; the speed at which the police officers had rushed him through the admittedly hostile crowd had caused him to trip and lose his balance. A Ministry spokesman went so far as to state that he was not pulled or dragged to the ground: 'The man is six foot three. It would take a fair bit of pulling.'

A report by Hugh Davies in the *Daily Telegraph* characterised many of the accounts of the evening:

Mr Heseltine, the Defence Secretary, was dragged to the ground in a tussle with anti-nuclear demonstrators at Newbury last night. Several women tried to punch and kick him.

The truth appears further down in his report:

He fell to the ground but was hoisted up by three police officers who, with the others, helped him barge his way into the building.

The *Daily Express*'s Colin Pratt, who was to become something of an expert on Greenham Common, produced this account:

As police formed a human chain around him, officers stumbled over some of the peace protestors lying on the steps of Newbury Town Hall. They fell to the ground dragging Heseltine with them. He was helped to his feet and ushered into the building.

Even the *Daily Mail* appears to have been doubtful about ascribing the 'dragging down' to the protestors:

Police formed a way through for Heseltine. Several women lay on the ground in front of the couple and when the police tried to guide the minister over them he was pulled to the ground.

At the very most the incident lasted thirty seconds. It was dark and there was considerable confusion. For the most part reporters did not feel hampered by these limitations, and although the accounts differed in many ways the *Times* and *Telegraph* confidently asserted that Heseltine was 'kicked and punched' while the *Daily Mail* said he 'appeared to be punched'.

The Press Council investigated complaints by women who had also been at Newbury Town Hall and produced some startlingly limp adjudications. In judgment on the Scottish *Daily Express*, the Council observed rather strangely that 'there could be more than one honest and accurate account and interpretation of what took place.' This is surely one of the most ludicrous statements that the Council has yet made. Either Mr Heseltine was, or was not, kicked, punched, dragged to the ground etc. There can be no equivocation here. If newspapers stated that he was physically abused when he himself said he was not, they were inaccurate and should be condemned as such. The only conclusion one can draw is that there was an expectation in the press that there would be some sort of incident and the reports fulfilled it regardless of what actually happened.

From that week in February onwards the publicity was unceasing and for the Greenham Common Women undesirable. There were reports of 'lesbian love-ins', 'cases of dysentery in the squalid camp', babies being born and taken into care by the Berkshire Health Authorities and court cases in which women were tried for obstruction, criminal damage and breaches of the peace. There was considerable attention paid to the feelings of the local residents, the complaints of the Thames Valley Police, who said that its resources were overstretched, and an anti-peace-camp group called Clean Up Newbury Town, tactfully referred to as Clean Up Newbury by the press. Of course much of what was reported was true, although one occasionally wonders where the reporters got their information. Take the exposé by Askold Krushelnycky in the *Mail on Sunday* of November 20 which was designed to show how the mindless occupants of the peace camp were manipulated by a trio of activists in London who dreamt up publicity stunts and suggested them to lieutenants in the camp. The story contained this paragraph:

Their last major move took seven months to plan. It was the operation where 130 women overnight became armed with boltcutters on an assault on the nine-mile barbed wire topped perimeter fence. Money had been collected to buy or hire the cutters. There was even a large cardigan sale to raise money.

This mention of a cardigan sale is most illuminating, for the Greenham Common Women never planned or held a cardigan sale. They say they used the phrase in telephone conversations between supporters in London as a code for the acquisition of the boltcutters. Could the *Mail on Sunday* have obtained its information from someone who had been listening in?

Many newspapers relied on personal accounts of life at Greenham Common camps provided, naturally, by their own women staff reporters. They exhibited different levels of contempt and bias and broadly reflected the attitudes of each newspaper. So the *Sun*'s undercover girl at the camp, Jean Ritchie, concentrated on the lesbian angle: 'Greenham is a lesbian community – four out of five are lesbians united in their hatred of men.'

She went on to describe the sort of treatment that the troops guarding the bases would mete out to the Greenham Common women:

If women are prepared to die, the paratroopers who turn their searchlights on Blue Gate are prepared to kill them.

'I joined the army to kill people. It's a sport innit,' says one of them.

'If they'd give us weapons we'd shoot you lot and a f - - - ing good thing that would be.

'If it weren't for you we could be in action now, killing people in Northern Ireland.'

By contrast Anne Robinson of the *Daily Mirror* took a rather more tolerant and open-minded view:

I didn't find myself among a group of lesbian subversives. Most of the women I could just as easily have bumped into in a bus queue. . . What Greenham Common women suffer from more than anything else is a distorted public image and they are too proud and weary to improve it.

Ann Leslie of the *Daily Mail* wrote a most clever and incisive piece which perfectly expressed the *Mail*'s suburban contempt for idealism. She concluded with this sentiment:

Any attempt to discuss defence issues in a realistic way results in them taking refuge in buzz words and phrases inherited from the soft-minded fall out of the Me Decade, 'using ones power assertively', 'taking responsibility for one's own life' and 'making a statement for life against death' etc. etc.

They seem to feel that, when in difficulty the solution is to pull down over their heads, like the woolly hats they all wear, some woolly phrase and its woolly warmth through their woolly minds and everything will come out right again.

. . . Clap hands, children of all ages everywhere. Tinkerbell is alive and well and living in Greenham Common and wearing a woolly hat.

The *Daily Express*, a little late in the day, joined the undercover school of journalism and sent Sarah Bond to spend two weeks at the camp, which fortuitously fell at the time of an eviction. Hints of sympathy appeared in Miss Bond's account of her uncomfortable fortnight but on the whole she opted for the view that most peace women were lesbian:

A lot of women go gay after arriving at the camp. With no men around they turn to each other for comfort. Other lesbians masquerade as peace women and go to Greenham just for sex because it is one of the few places where they can be open about it.

A 19-year-old girl told me, 'I turned gay after I got here. But I'm not a man-hater and I freaked out the first time I slept with a woman.'

'If you're not a dike in this world you're punished by coming back as a man,' said one, 'or a monkey,' added another with a snigger.

The single greatest fiction about the Greenham peace camp appeared on August 20, 1983, in the *Daily Express*, the newspaper, you will remember, that showed such determination in discrediting the People's March for Jobs. I reproduce most of the article by Colin Pratt and

Michael Evans to demonstrate what little evidence the *Daily Express* demands of its reporters.

REVEALED: THE SPY IN THE CAMP. RED MOLE SHOCK AT GREENHAM. PEACE WOMEN WERE TIPPED OFF OVER TOP SECRET DELIVERY ran the headline:

Security chiefs are hunting a Red Mole buried deep inside the Greenham Common Cruise base.

The infiltrator is feeding secret information to the 'peace' women camped outside, it was revealed last night.

There had been growing suspicions over the way the women seem to know what is going on in the base.

Now the authorities have proof of the mole's existence. It emerged this week when the women were tipped off about an early morning lorry delivery of non-nuclear missile casings.

Only six people inside the base were supposed to have known the date and timing of the top secret delivery from a nearby arms factory.

The civilian driver signed the Official Secrets Act forbidding him to talk about his load. But when he turned into the entrance at 8.30 am he found his path blocked by a hostile human barricade.

He was the only lorry the demonstrators tried to block this week. And from the insults they hurled at him and at police battling to get through, it was clear the women knew what the vehicle contained.

An official said yesterday: 'The possibility of someone inside sympathetic to the women's cause passing them tit bits has been known for some time. But this is something else, it had implications.

A friend of the lorry driver said he was only given his delivery instructions at the last minute and he swears he told no-one.

This is one more piece of evidence that these demonstrators have a total grip on the place.

The Greenham women are strongly linked to the Left through their ties with CND, the Workers' Revolutionary Party and other similar groups.

A Russian TV crew often film the demonstrators outside the Berkshire base. Copies of the communist paper the Morning Star circulate at the women's camp.

Local residents have become angry and frustrated by the lack of official action to clear out the women who have been camped there for two years.

There is a long list of grievances. Many parts of the gorse and bracken-covered common around the camp are totally polluted because there is not proper sanitation for the women.

There have been bitter complaints about the women using the showers at Newbury Leisure centre for their weekly baths. One local mother said, 'They stand in the showers with their under-clothes so that they get clean themselves and do their laundry at the same time.'

'If we did that there would be an outcry and we'd be banned.'

Recently some of the women have started to wash while naked in full view of the married quarters at the base.

Let us perform a little dissection on the Pratt–Evans effort. The first four paragraphs are unsupported statements of fact, so we have to look further to find the evidence on which they base these extraordinary claims. This, it turns out, is remarkably slim. All they have found to support the RED MOLE SHOCK is the circumstantial detail that one lorry was singled out by the women for a demonstration. There is a quote from an official but he only admits to the possibility of someone passing tit-bits of information, not the fact of them doing so. And then there is the useful quotation from the friend of the lorry driver which more or less sums up the *Daily Express*'s view. Considerable claims are made without proof and all the participants of the story, the lorry driver, the official and the lorry driver's friend are unidentified. From this point Pratt and Evans proceed to knock the Greenham Common women for their supposed relations with the Workers' Revolutionary Party and their filthy habits.

I found this story fascinating, and the more so when the Press Council published the results of its own investigations some seven months later. For neither Michael Heseltine, Peter Imbert, the local

Chief Constable, nor the Newbury District Council had any record of any of the events that the *Daily Express* described in its front-page story. Was the lorry and its secret cargo of missile casings really non-existent? What is more, the local Director for Environmental Services said that he did not think a public health nuisance had been created by the camp, while his colleague, the Director of Recreations Services, said that there had been only one complaint of a peace camp woman taking a shower in her underclothes. Remember, all these people are in one way or another opposed to the Greenham Common Peace Camp and had every reason to support the *Daily Express* story.

In view of these damning denials the new editor of the *Express*, Sir Larry Lamb, displayed a quite sensational obstinacy.

His representative at the Press Council, Morris Bennet, said that Sir Larry saw 'no reason to withdraw, apologise or qualify any matters complained of and furthermore that he did not wish to enter into debate with the women and give them further publicity. He remained satisfied that the story was accurate.' The Council replied that it was untrue and that the delivery of missile casings did not take place. Following publication of the Press Council's decision, which was considerably foreshortened in the *Daily Express*, the paper printed the following.

The Press Council says, inter alia, that a *Daily Express* story about the so-called peace women at Greenham Common was untrue.

Not so. The *Daily Express* is quite satisfied that it was accurate.

The Press Council also says that the story was such that it should have been very carefully researched, checked and cross-checked. We have news for them. It was.

It will surprise no one that the Press Council was unable to confirm the story from its own sources. If newspapers relied upon such official sources they would not make meaningful disclosures of any kind at any time.

Remember the *Daily Express*'s sources? A nameless official and a lorry driver's friend. Hardly the sort of impressive investigative journalism that the *Daily Express* hints was behind this story. Anyway, let us proceed:

The Press Council's failure to confirm what we have discovered does not entitle that body to accuse the *Daily Express*
reporters of telling lies.

It is true that we refused the Greenham Common women the
opportunity to reply, at enormous length, to the story.

Even the Press Council will presumably be able to appreciate
that the reply the Greenham Common mob sought to have
published was designed solely to secure further publicity for their
nefarious activities.

We would prefer to take the Press Council seriously. But they
make it difficult.

The refusal to give Greenham Common women further publicity is, in
my opinion, a pose so transparent that one is vaguely surprised that even
the *Daily Express* had the gall to print it. Three weeks later Sir Larry
Lamb's paper ran the Exclusive and compelling dossier by Undercover
Girl Sarah Bond on the Camp That Declared War on Men which was
nothing if not 'further publicity for their nefarious activities'. Of course,
it was the sort of publicity that Sir Larry was quite content to give the
Greenham Common women; unfavourable and biased. But the real
point here, and I think it began to emerge in the discussion of the *Daily
Express* story about the Duchess of Kent's 'electro-convulsive therapy',
is that the paper is willing to run a sensational story on the flimsiest of
evidence and then, when it is exposed, will go on insisting that it is right;
that the *Daily Express* is a proud and fearless organisation that will not
shrink from the truth; and that people of Britain may continue to place
their trust in the integrity, honesty and uprightness of its employees.
The above reaction was the only feasible response to the Press Council.
It would simply have been too embarrassing to attempt to counter the
statements of Heseltine and Imbert.

The Press Council also made some comments on an editorial that the
Daily Express carried on the day of the original report, describing it,
somewhat mildly, as abusive and unjustified. The newspaper was so
anxious to attack the Peace Camp on the grounds that it was a waste of
taxpayers' money, that it was a threat to British security, and that it was
an unsightly nuisance, that Pratt and Evans's story must have seemed

like a gift. If it had wanted to construct a news story to fit an editorial it could hardly have done better. Here is the editorial:

SWEEP AWAY THIS TIP

Official feebleness over the women's so-called 'peace' camp at Greenham Common is disgraceful.

When on earth is the government going to DO something? After two years, and within weeks of the scheduled arrival of the first cruise missiles, this grubby commune is still being allowed to create a major public nuisance at the taxpayer's expense.

Worse, as the *Daily Express* today reveals on Page One, there is now every reason to believe that they have a dangerous anti-western anti-British 'mole' actually inside the base.

Of course, the cause of peace is vital. Of course, the cause of one-sided disarmament is a perfectly honourable, if misguided cause.

But the women of Greenham, with their mindless zealotry and tireless exhibitionism, have succeeded only in damaging that cause.

They were at first appealing – until we all began to realise just how suspect their motives were. Then they became repulsive.

Now, alas, for those of us lucky enough not to have them on our doorstep, they are merely boring. But it would be dangerous to ignore them in the hope that they will go away.

Their slatternly, disease-prone tip should be swept away and soon. The storing of nuclear weapons is a serious business to say the least.

Surely it is not beyond the government's ingenuity to devise legislation which ensures no pack of mindless mischievous militants, of whatever sex, is allowed within miles of a nuclear base.

The crucial sentences for our purposes are 'they were at first appealing until we all began to realise just how suspect their motives were. Then they became repulsive.' In other words, while the peace camp was a quaint novelty, the *Daily Express* was happy to be fair in its treatment, but when the Women's message became a little too insistent and their support a little too widespread the paper's attitude changed. True, the women's publicity gimmicks had become tedious, but there was no actual change in attitude or behaviour that justified the adjectival swing from 'appealing' to 'repulsive'. They had always been quite clear about their motives, or, to use a less sinister word, aims.

The most regrettable part of this editorial is the spirit of intolerance that it betrays. One is reminded of *Pravda*. People may put a point of view when the *Daily Express* judges it to be agreeable or harmless, but as soon as an opinion acquires credibility and support and threatens to change things against the paper's wishes then the *Daily Express*, sometime champion of individual rights, calls for legislation to sweep away the 'slatternly tip'. More importantly, this attitude, which is increasingly to be found in the popular press of the right, is the first step towards tyranny. The result is non-existent lorries loaded with non-existent missile casings and non-existent demonstrations inspired by information from non-existent moles.

CHAPTER 7

Hilda Ogden Mugged
by Martians

Great areas of woodland are cut down each day with no other object than to engage lightly the mind of the British newspaper reader on his or her way to work. It is a sad idea, particularly when you consider how feeble and transitory is the entertainment that newspapers seek to give us: the competitions that are near impossible to win, the horoscopes that do not predict, the diets that do not slim, the puzzles that would not test the competence of a baboon and the many stories and articles that do not inform but merely feed off the pre-eminent medium of television in the hope of maintaining the reader's interest between one evening's viewing and the next. It is even sadder when one discovers that the same dishonesty which characterises so much of Fleet Street's handling of the news is also to be found in the froth of newspapers, those sections intended merely to amuse the reader.

It is nowhere more difficult to make the distinction between news and entertainment than in the area of show business and television reporting. This is something I knew little about until I interviewed a television writer whose principal duty was to cover soap operas, or 'sudsology' as one newspaper described it, but was also available for light duties in other parts of the beat. He had no hesitation in estimating that two out of every five of his contributions contained a substantial element of fiction; he was far less adventurous than his colleagues on rival newspapers, he added. His fictions ranged from a simple fabricated quote to an entire interview. The latter would probably include some true facts and quotes from previous interviews (which are themselves unreliable in the extreme) but would mostly be made up after a refreshing lunch.

He gave me an example of how it is done: 'Say a film star like James Coburn flies into London to promote a new film during the Wimbledon tennis tournament. Well, obviously you've got to put the two events together. So I'd write something on the lines of: Tough guy James Coburn never misses the centre court thrills. He has a clause written into his contract which stipulates that he has the Wimbledon fortnight off every year – no matter what he is doing or where he is in the world. Then I'd bung in a few harmless quotes and mention the film that he is here to promote. Naturally it is all made up but I guarantee that nobody will complain, least of all Coburn or his agent, who would probably be pleased that the film has got some publicity: the paper is more or less happy and I suppose the reader is mildly interested.'

He is right. The complaints from well-known victims of these reports are few and far between. Occasionally someone like Mick Jagger will protest that the *Daily Star* has made up an interview with him, but generally the sheer volume of fabrication is such that the business of making representations to the newspaper or the Press Council would take up too much time. An exception is John Cleese, who successfully appealed to the Press Council over remarks he was reported to have made by the *Sun*. He recalls that he has received much the same sort of treatment from the self-righteous *Daily Mirror*: 'A director asked me to re-read a film script by a young writer. In order to encourage me he sent it round with a pot of caviar. I thanked him politely but declined to accept the script. Some weeks later the *Daily Mirror* wrote a story which had me saying the script was crap and feeding the caviar to the dog. It was absolutely untrue and extremely hurtful to the young writer.'

The *Daily Mirror* presumably found the story credible since the behaviour described is what we have come to expect of Cleese, or rather of his television persona of the manic hotel proprietor Basil Fawlty. And here is the rub. It is this confusion between the actor himself and his screen character that is so often responsible for distortion and fabrication. If an actor does not behave in the way that is consistent with his best-known roles then the journalist arranges things so that he does.

For the sake of the journalists' sanity one hopes, for once, that this behaviour is entirely deliberate.

However, when one considers the greatest confusion of 1983 in this area, one wonders. This was the coverage of *Coronation Street*, which regularly attracts more viewers than Labour voters in a General Election and was once described by the Poet Laureate, Sir John Betjeman, as the best social drama since Dickens serialised *Pickwick Papers*. Granada TV has not divined the reason for the national press's extraordinary obsession with *Coronation Street* but it believes that it may have been caused by a survey of readers' preferences conducted by a Sunday newspaper in 1982 which found that they were prepared to digest any amount of nonsense as long as it was vaguely connected with the programme. Conveniently for Fleet Street there was a number of incidents in the lives of the cast which enabled journalists to create an off-screen soap opera containing as much energy and invention as the programme itself: Mr Peter Adamson (Len Fairclough) was charged with assaulting two small girls in a swimming pool and later acquitted; Violet Carson (Ena Sharples), Jack Howarth (Albert Tatlock) and Peter Dudley (Bert Tilsley) died; Doris Speed (Annie Walker) suffered a prolonged illness; Pat Phoenix (Elsie Tanner) was stricken with pleurisy and then left the series; and Anne Kirkbride (Deirdre Barlow) was prosecuted for possessing cannabis. Mildly interesting though these events might have been, they were not very significant in the great scheme of things; certainly none deserved the front-page stories sprinkled with words like 'shock', 'drama', 'trauma', 'disaster' and 'tragedy'. This is the vocabulary of airline crashes and terrorist outrages, not of the comings and goings of the cast of a soap opera.

The confusion was total since all the headlines announcing the real-life events used the screen names; thus I'M STAYING IN THE STREET SAYS LEN (*Daily Mirror*) and DRUG CASE DEIRDRE AXED BY CO-OP (*Sun*). Newspapers seemed to lose all sense of reality. The *Sun* for example replaced such tantalising stories as BIG MAC BOY KILLED BY LAUGHING KNIFE MANIAC and RIDDLE OF WIFE IN DEATH RIDE ON M1 with HILDA OGDEN MUGGED. Was this the preview of some future script in which the indomitable Mrs Ogden is set upon, or did it refer to an event which actually had taken place? The answer is that Jean Alexander, not Hilda Ogden, had been robbed of a wedding ring; not, of course, her own ring but the brass prop she wore in the role of Stan Ogden's wife. Is this worth banner headlines on the front page? Sometimes this confusion seemed to affect the actors. An exclusive in the *News of the World* by Ivan Waterman revealed how the scriptwriter was going to deal with Peter Adamson, who had been dismissed by Granada for selling his story to the *Sun*. Under the headline WHAT A CHEAP AND NASTY ENDING Waterman wrote:

Actor Peter Adamson last night accused Coronation Street bosses of plotting a sex smear campaign against him.

Adamson, who was fired from the show after 22 years playing Len Fairclough, stormed, 'They cast me aside, kicked me in the head in public. Now they are going to rub my nose in the dirt. They have sunk beneath the lowest common denominator – gone as low as they can. They're petty minded, malicious people.'

Next Wednesday millions of viewers will learn of Len's death in a mystery car crash when his van careers off a motorway into a bridge.

But Adamson says that future storylines will suggest he was having a secret affair . . .

He said of his TV death and the secret affair, 'Its nothing more than a cheap, ridiculous smear campaign. Their motive is to blacken my name even further. They want any sympathy the fans had for me to be destroyed – to make the name of Fairclough a dirty word.

Of course the idea that Granada were plotting a 'sex smear campaign' against Adamson is preposterous, and even if they were doing so against the fictional character of Len Fairclough it would hardly reflect on Mr Adamson himself. And yet the *News of the World* saw fit to use this remarkable misapprehension in a prominent position in the news pages. On other occasions the reporters themselves were obviously muddled. The *Sun*, for instance, reported that the actor Fred Feast had been the subject of a routine police inquiry. Throughout its account of this very minor incident, the paper referred to Fred Feast as Fred Gee, the name of the character he plays in the programme.

The situation was not helped by the fact that concurrent with these real-life dramas the plot of the serial had been hotted up somewhat by an affair between the characters Deirdre Barlow and Mike Baldwin. This became the subject of considerable debate in the press. All manner of expert was consulted, feature-writers were instructed to probe into the agony of the cuckolded party (Ken Barlow) and there was constant speculation as to whether Deirdre and Mike had or had not made love. For the minority of the population who do not watch the programme the headlines were utterly bemusing. Even *The Times* found space in its precious news pages to announce: DEIRDRE AND MIKE LEFT DANCING IN THE DARK.

The most amusing and, indeed, the most surreal part of Fleet Street's obsession with *Coronation Street* was the way in which it sought to explain the crisis which had hit the programme, a crisis which journalists themselves had largely created. The *Daily Mirror* consulted its astrologer, June Penn, and asked her to plot the zodiacal charts of the characters – using, of course, the fictional birthdays. What value there was in using dates plucked out of the scriptwriters' head one cannot imagine; still, the *Daily Mirror* was sufficiently impressed with the idea to devote its centre page spread to Miss Penn's conclusions. The *Sunday Mirror* excelled itself in an exclusive feature by Tom Hendry and Ian Smith which stated that *Coronation Street*'s troubles could all be traced to the use of a rehearsal block which was situated at the intersection of two ley lines.

It is not surprising that such an extravagant muddle led to a considerable number of outright lies which should in no way be mitigated by the trivial nature of the subject. Norman Frisby, the luckless individual who is charged with handling the press for Granada, summed up Fleet Street's attitude at the height of the obsession: 'They make things up and when you tell them they are not true they turn it into a row.' Naturally enough the *Sun* led the way with some startlingly absurd stories, the most outrageous of which appeared on September 10, 1983: 'TV stars are queuing up to take the place of Peter Adamson in Coronation Street. Everyone from Russell Harty to a *Crossroads* star wants in on the act. Even Lord Olivier has said he would be thrilled to appear.'

One could, perhaps, see Russell Harty in the role of the loutish Fairclough but that Olivier would give up what appears to be a pretty established career in the theatre and films to spend the rest of his days on the *Coronation Street* set is doubtful. It was the *Sun* which also broke the news that the Queen had phoned Buckingham Palace from Mexico to plead with the staff to put vital episodes of *Coronation Street* on a video recorder so that she could catch up on her return from the American Royal Tour. All the evidence that the newspaper could muster to support the story was that 'the Queen is an avid fan of the Street' and that there was a video recorder somewhere in the palace. It goes without saying that Buckingham Palace did not confirm the telephone call, which was the whole point of the story. On another occasion the *Sun* turned its attention to Christabel Finch, who plays Ken and Deirdre Barlow's six-year-old daughter, Tracey. The paper discovered that Christabel's home was empty and the little actress had 'gone missing'. This, of course, was untrue, since she was quite safe with parents who were looking for another house; she was only 'missing' because the *Sun* could not find her. Eventually the newspaper tracked her down and took a photograph which was printed the next day accompanied by the headline THE SUN FINDS TRACEY.

Norman Frisby recorded the newspaper's behaviour when it was learnt that Doris Speed (Annie Walker) was unwell. 'It was claimed that she collapsed. Not once, but twice. She had been rushed to hospital and she had a mystery illness. It was only a mystery illness to the newspaper because Doris would not want us to tell them what was actually wrong with her. She had not collapsed. There had been no rushing to hospital. Doris was not seriously ill. She needed peace and quiet.' The paper apparently took this last phrase as an invitation to send one of its representatives to sit on her doorstep.

The fiction in the coverage of *Coronation Street* was small beer compared with the lengths to which Rupert Murdoch's popular papers went to beguile their readership. The *News of the World*, under the editorship of Derek Jameson, obviously decided that if fiction sold newspapers science fiction would sell a good deal more. In June 1983, while the rest of us were absorbed by the General Election, the paper turned to extra-terrestrial matters. Under the headline CLOSE ENCOUNTER AT THE SHAMROCK CAFE, Keith Beabey and Pippa Sibley revealed that three women had been kidnapped by a UFO after they had spent a pleasant evening together near Wolverhampton. It started like this:

Strange red and white lights hovered overhead as three women drove home from their weekly night out.

Mysteriously their car came to a halt outside the Shamrock Cafe on the A5 in Shropshire, though the driver had her foot hard down on the accelerator.

Then the lights suddenly vanished and the trio rushed excitedly to a nearby police station, where they reported a close encounter with a UFO.

But that was when they noticed something even stranger happening. The drive to the police station should have taken five minutes. Instead it took twenty-five.

Only now, with the help of hypnosis, under the strictest supervision, has an explanation been found for those twenty missing minutes. And it is amazing.

Each of the women has independently told the same story that they did have a close encounter, far closer than they first imagined. For each says that she was taken aboard a spacecraft, examined by alien beings and then released.

The paper then reproduced the accounts of each of the three women, Rosemary Hawkins, Valerie Walters and Viv Hayward. Here is Rosemary's:

Bright lights. White tinged with yellow and red. So strange its three. No sound.

We are frightened the lights are attached to a spacecraft of some kind.

I am floating and I'm not in the car any more with Viv or Val, I feel big and bloated.

It's a semi-circular room. I'm on a bed in the room like a long
table on a stand.

There's something coming. I can hear them. Something is in
the room. Its metal. It doesn't walk it sort of rolls on wheels.

It's about four feet tall, round on the top with a round body and
round legs.

It's looking at me. There's more coming. It's the same noise.
There are four. They are around me.

They haven't got a face. Their heads move up and down.
That's how I know they are talking to me.

They don't seem to be nasty. They just want to have a look. I
feel so relaxed and they feel friendly. I like them.

By contrast Viv found the aliens rather frightening. They put their
hands inside her legs and pulled her bones about a bit and then released
her. She described them thus: 'They are four feet tall. They have no
hair. They are ugly. They have strange looking noses; thin arms I can't
see their legs. They are dressed in green cloaks.'

Later in the story Rosemary suggests that the aliens had singled out
her and her friends because each possessed a radically different
personality, thus presenting the aliens with a good cross-section of the
human mentality.

This entertaining scoop was accompanied by an equally entertaining
drawing of one of the women being examined by those curious little
beings from another world, who anyone who used to read *Eagle* would
recognise. As far as I remember your average Martian is always made of
metal, favours the colour green, never has a face, is unfailingly
inquisitive and is always lacking in stature. Tempting though it was to
entertain the idea that a flying saucer had landed near the Shamrock
Cafe on the A5, everyone chose to ignore the *News of the World*'s
revelations.

Undaunted, in October the paper announced: UFO LANDS IN
SUFFOLK – AND THAT'S OFFICIAL. Mr Keith Beabey it was, again,
who wrote:

A UFO has landed in Britain – and that staggering fact has
been officially confirmed.

Despite a massive cover-up *News of the World* investigators have proof that the mysterious craft came to earth in a red ball of light at 3am on December 27, 1980.

It happened in a pine forest called Tangham Wood just half a mile away from the United States Air Force base at RAF Woodbridge in Suffolk.

An American airman who was there told us there were beings in silver space suits aboard the craft.

Farm cattle and forest animals ran berserk as the spacecraft, a sloping silver dish about 20ft across its base, silently glided to land in a blinding explosion of lights.

About 200 military and civilian personnel, British and American, witnessed the event. The airman said the visitors appeared to be expected.

Can the *News of the World* really believe that none of its readers have seen *Close Encounters of the Third Kind?* Obviously. The two main witnesses to the event are a man named 'Art Wallace', a junior airman whose identity is protected by the *News of the World* for 'security reasons' and Lt Colonel Charles Halt, deputy commander of the USAF 81st Tactical Fighter Wing stationed at Woodbridge. The latter filed a report to his superiors which went as follows:

Early in the morning two USAF security police patrolmen saw unusual lights outside the back gate of Woodbridge.

Thinking an aircraft might have crashed or been forced down they called for permission to go outside the gate to investigate.

The on-duty flight chief allowed three patrolmen to proceed on foot.

The individuals reported seeing a strange glowing object in the forest.

The object was described as being metallic in appearance and triangular in shape, approximately two to three metres across the base and approximately two metres high. It illuminated the entire forest with a white light.

The object itself had a pulsating red light on top and a bank of blue lights underneath. The object was hovering on legs. As the patrolmen approached the object it manoeuvred through the trees and disappeared.

At the time the animals on a nearby farm went into a frenzy. The object was sighted approximately an hour later near the back gate.

The next day three depressions one and a half inches deep and seven inches in diameter were found where the object had been sighted on the ground.

Later on during the night a red sunlike light was seen through the trees. It moved about and pulsated. At one point it appeared to throw off glowing particles and then broke into five separate white objects and disappeared.

Immediately thereafter the red starlike objects were noted in the sky, two objects in the North and one in the South, all of which were about 10 degrees above the horizon. The objects moved rapidly and displayed green-blue lights. The objects in the North appeared elliptical through an 8–12 power lens.

They turned full circle. The objects in the North remained in the sky for an hour or more. The objects in the South were visible for two or three hours and beamed down a storm of lights from time to time.

Inside, the newspaper carried a startling interview with 'Art Wallace' who said that he had seen a craft with a green light on top and that he understood from his fellow patrolmen that there were little men inside wearing silver suits.

This time the *News of the World* was not entirely ignored. Adrian Berry, the level-headed Science Editor of the *Daily Telegraph*, wrote that he too had found a UFO and produced a picture of it hovering over St Paul's cathedral in London. He wrote: 'Our photographer Paul Armiger was standing beside St Paul's when this huge spacecraft came roaring over his head. He knew its occupant must have flown all the way from Alpha Centauri to kidnap the Dean . . . '

He went on to suggest that the *News of the World*'s 'evidence' was, if anything, less convincing. He continued:

All that had happened was that an United States Air Force

Colonel at RAF Woodbridge had seen an unexplained light in the surrounding woods. This could only have been the rotating beam of Orford Ness lighthouse. The only problem when one looks into these stories is that usually the town cannot be found on any map and never existed, and the scientists did not utter a word of what they are quoted as saying, their remarks having been invented by unscrupulous reporters. . . . Would alien visitors really seek information about humanity from the dullest and least reliable of mankind? Would they really rush about in disc-shaped vehicles with abysmal aerodynamic qualities?

Derek Jameson wrote to the *Daily Telegraph* to defend his paper's exclusive story, drawing Berry's attention to the depression mentioned in the Colonel's report. Berry had an answer for this too, which he was kind enough to share with us through the Letters column of his own paper: 'Mr Thurkettle, a Forestry Commission official, who examined the site, has attributed the depressions to rabbits. The local police say that they were probably made by an animal.'

Berry had used the word impudence to describe the *News of the World*'s report; it is hard to disagree. Here was a newspaper claiming that there had been official verification when there had been none, and that two hundred people had been expecting the landing when only one could be found to talk about it – and even he wanted to remain anonymous.

The following Sunday the paper returned to the subject by revealing that there had been a SINISTER PLOT TO HUSH UP THE TRUTH. A section was devoted to our friend 'Art Wallace', who, it turns out, had tried to re-enlist with the air force but had been rejected because there was no record of his first term of service. He is quoted as saying that he may have been drugged and brainwashed.

With the country crawling with little silver men and the skies crowded with unidentified craft the *News of the World*'s sister paper, the *Sun*, eventually decided to ask the question that must have been at the back of many minds: IS YOUR NEIGHBOUR FROM OUTER SPACE? With the help of an UFO investigator named Brad Steiger and a theoretical biologist, Dr Thomas Easton, they gave eight telltale tip-offs that can give an alien away: (1) They sleep and work unusual hours because an alien's day on his native planet may be shorter or longer than ours; (2) They show anxiety, stress or discomfort when using earth transportation; (3) They read a lot of newspapers and magazines with the view to gaining as much information about the planet Earth as possible; (4) They own unusually large amounts of high-technology equipment; (5) They misuse common everyday objects such as food-mixers and vacuum cleaners; (6) They have homes with ill-matching decorative schemes; (7) They have an unusual object on the home which is highly regarded and protected which 'could be a device that is from the alien's planet and is used for communication'. The thought occurs that, with the possible exception of the third, all these tip-offs could equally well identify the typical *Sun* reader. The paper then appealed to its readers to write in and tell them about any aliens who might have moved in next door. The response, sadly, seems to have been small.

But perhaps one is being unjust in ridiculing this particular range of fiction from the Bouverie Street dream factory. The UFO articles were all commissioned in the belief that they would amuse the readership, which to an extent they must have. The only mistake seems to be for journalists like Derek Jameson to state in public that they believed their own stories.

In the same way one does not expect editors to believe in the predictions of the astrologers who feature so conspicuously in the popular press. For instance, the *Sun*'s astrologer (Sunshine Stargazer) until early 1983, Suzie Elliot, specialised in oblique hints about horses to back, advice on handling children and the reader's love-life. Her predictions for Taurus on January 3, 1983, possess a remarkably close bearing on her own life: 'Bring pressure on people who are untidy with words . . . avoid repeating yourself.'

Within a matter of days Suzie was sacked by the editor, Kelvin Mackenzie, for repeating herself. In short she was recycling her predictions so that Tuesday's advice for Capricorns would turn up word for word as Friday's advice for Pisceans. The honesty of the approach is debatable, though it is a sensibly economical way of going about the business of tabloid astrology. Alan Rusbridger, the *Guardian*'s excellent diarist, made some investigations into the methods employed by the Sunshine Stargazer. I quote part of them:

Suzie is married to one Roger Elliot, stargazer for the *News of the World*. It has been remarked that Suzie and Roger are often at one in their prognostications. I tackled Mr Elliot on the point. 'The line is very bad,' he tells me. 'Do you write your wife's column?' I persist. 'Sorry, can't hear you,' he says.

He tells me how his wife and he employ a word-processor to help them in their work and that the mistakes in Suzie's column were caused by a computer error. He tells me that he is most put out that Mr Mackenzie has sacked him so precipitously.

'So it's you he's sacked?' I asked him. 'Sorry, the line's gone very faint again,' he says. 'It's you he's sacked,' I bellow. 'Yes,' he says.

After Rusbridger's story I delved into the cuttings library to find that there was indeed a remarkable similarity between Suzie's predictions each day, and that there also was unanimity in the Elliot household about the areas of suitable advice (children, horse racing and love-life). Still, whether Mr Elliot composed the lot or whether it was the fault of the computer, which had been programmed to spew out three weeks of forecasts so that the Elliots could enjoy a long winter break, does not seem to matter. But Mr Mackenzie, clearly a man of principle when it comes to astrology, felt that his readers should receive fresh predictions each day and insisted that Suzie should go.

In her stead he appointed a professional astrologer, June Howard Baker, who teaches the subject at Watford Technical College. Her predictions were to prove reliable, or at least original, and for a while everyone at the *Sun* was happy. This state of affairs lasted until the dying days of 1983, when Mrs Howard Baker was asked to consult her charts and come up with some conclusions about 1984. When the predictions arrived at Bouverie Street it was felt by the sub-editors that they were, not to put too fine a point on it, extremely dull. So an imaginative mind was employed to inject a little zest into them. Thus we were to read that Princess Diana was to have a difficult pregnancy and

Frank Sinatra was to suffer a heart attack and undergo an emergency by-pass operation.

And then there is bingo and all its low-minded variations. The game was introduced to Fleet Street some three years ago and has since become the main area in which the national dailies compete for circulation. The attraction for newspapers is that bingo builds up sales over a long period, unlike the one-off competition; the reader has to buy a particular newspaper each day to check the numbers on the card he has received through his letterbox. This process of checking is legally defined as a skill, which is important for newspapers since it distinguishes the game from the simple lottery, which would be against the law. The attraction to the reader is also considerable; not only does the game require the absolute minimum of intelligence but there is also the lure of literally millions of pounds.

Sadly these millions have proved as bogus as the rest of the contents of this great free press of ours. Take the *Daily Express*'s Millionaire's Club, which was started in September 1983 by Sir Larry Lamb, whose instinct for vulgar entertainment is as sure as it was during the decade of his editorship at the *Sun*. The paper had us all believing that there was a very real chance of winning a million pounds by buying the newspaper every day and filling in our cards. The effect of Sir Larry's game was quite astonishing. In July 1983 the *Daily Express* was only 45,000 ahead of its chief rival, the *Daily Mail*. After the introduction of the Millionaires Club the gap increased to 297,586 copies. Other Fleet Street newspapers were forced to follow. The *Mail* introduced the Millionaires Mail and the *Daily Star*, *Daily Mirror* and the *Sun* either introduced new games or pepped up their existing competitions, so that by November an estimated thirty million pounds was on offer in the national press.

The newspapers betrayed their low motives by sniping at each other. The *Daily Express* ridiculed the *Daily Mail*'s imitation, the *Sun* printed the *Daily Express* numbers ('Why waste £1.08 a week on the fading *Daily Express* just to check the Millionaires Club numbers? The *Sun* will give the service free'). The *Standard* retaliated by printing the *Sun*'s bingo numbers. The *Daily Star* and *Daily Mirror* devoted large areas of their front pages to claiming that the nation was gripped by bingo fever.

Meanwhile the *Observer*, in the shape of Peter Durisch, took a long cool look at the chances of winning of some of these games. He consulted Professor Mervyn Stone of the Department of Statistical Science at University College London, who first set about calculating the odds of winning the competition which had started it all, the *Daily Express*'s Millionaires Club:

'If you allow ten possible digits in each possible position then that gives a million numbers,' he said. 'If the winning numbers are drawn at random, then the probability of a particular person winning on a particular day is one chance in a million million.

'If we assume that two million readers are doing the competition, then the chance of any one of them winning on a particular day is one in 500,000.

'If we assume that these readers all check their cards six days a week for a year, then the chance of winning in that year is 500,000 divided by 312 (six days times 52 weeks) which is one chance in 1,603.

Thus, assuming the winning numbers are random, then statistically you could expect a winner every 1,603 years.

By contrast the *Daily Mail*'s game offered exceptionally good odds; Professor Stone estimated that the paper would, given all the assumptions he made in the *Daily Express* calculation, create a millionaire every 400 years, which is very probably why the shrewd fellows at Carmelite House took out insurance against this eventuality. It was as well that the *Daily Mail* paid out £250,000 to one reader, since a fortnight before, when the competition was launched, Fleet Street had gloatingly reported that thousands of readers had claimed secondary prizes of toasters. The *Daily Mirror* reported that because of a mistake in the cards some 250,000 toasters, worth three million pounds, would have to be dispatched at huge cost to every hamlet in the country. The *Mirror*'s enjoyment of the *Mail*'s embarrassment seems to have got the better of its reporters, and a more reliable figure of 900 toasters was produced by the *Guardian*. Still, it was a painful episode for the *Daily Mail*, which only two years before had caused some 8,000 people to think that they had won the same prize of £35,000. Many of them made their claims in person causing sizable congestion in Carmelite Street.

The proprietors of the two main protagonists in the bingo war, Lord Rothermere of the *Daily Mail* and Lord Matthews of the *Express* Group, did not appear to be over-enthusiastic about the competitions and the daft promotional material which they spawned. Rothermere is said to have described the Millionaire Mail as 'a bit of a con', while Lord Matthews was happy with the Millionaires Club as long as the million was not actually paid out. When asked by an executive if it might not be time for the paper to fulfil its promise and actually elect a member of the public to its club, Lord Matthews replied that he needed all his money to fend off potential takeover bids from the Australian magnate Robert Holmes A' Court, who has long had designs on the *Express* Group.

Lord Matthews might have mentioned that his company had recently paid a very considerable sum to the late Diana Dors, who was first employed as an agony aunt by the *Daily Star* and then as a dietician. Miss Dors, who after her international fame as a film star went into decline showed considerable aptitude for marketing herself and her books, signed up with the paper to compile an advice column on the lines of Miss Proops's feature in the *Daily Mirror*. The fee was £10,000, and the response from the paper's readership in the early months of 1983 was sufficient for the editor, Mr Lloyd Turner, and his executives to believe that the money had been well invested. They did not at this stage consider it odd that their agony aunt saw few of the letters that poured into the paper's offices in Manchester.

In reality the business of her column was almost totally conducted by a *Daily Star* executive and a secretary. The executive selected five or six letters, conveyed them to Miss Dors for her advice and then put her remarks into cogent journalese. The secretary, meanwhile, answered the many letters which were not chosen for publication. It goes without saying that this rather inadequate service bears no resemblance to the way in which agony aunts like Claire Rayner and Marje Proops normally operate. Before Mr Turner had time to address himself to the problem of providing a more honest advice column, Miss Dors and Mr

Dandy Kim Waterfield, her business partner, let it be known that come the spring of that year she would be willing to divulge her secret slimming plan.

Newspapers get very excited about this sort of thing, particularly when it is compiled by a well-known show-business name. Without seeing a single sample of the diet Lloyd Turner offered £17,000 for the Dors slimming plan, which was apparently to be called the X Cel Diet. Mr Waterfield, as any good businessman would, wondered if he might not extract a little more from the paper which had made the mistake of declaring its enthusiasm. He let it be known that another national daily was willing to pay as much as £25,000 for the diet. The *Daily Star*'s reaction must have exceeded all Mr Waterfield's expectations; they promptly offered £42,000, to be paid in instalments of £3,300. Added to this the paper agreed to pay a straight fee of £6,000 to Miss Dors for the colour photographs they would use of her during the serialisation of her diet. Mr Waterfield was also guaranteed free advertising for the promotion of the spin-off products from the diet.

At the same time he signed a similar contract with the fledgling breakfast TV company, TV-AM, which was estimated to be worth between £17,000 and £20,000. The *Daily Star* and TV-AM agreed that this would damage the interests of neither and came to an arrangement whereby they promoted each other's coverage of the Dors Diet.

As the days warmed to summer both organisations made themselves ready to receive the much-vaunted diet. The paper alerted its readers to its imminent arrival and began to receive a favourable response from them. But come the date of delivery there was an odd reluctance on the part of Miss Dors to release her material. A young feature writer, Sandra White, was detailed to extract the diet from the actress and to start planning its presentation. Eventually she was sent a bundle of recipes which Miss White quickly observed were by no stretch of the imagination a diet. The Sunday before the serialisation was due to begin she telephoned her editor to break the news. He seems to have been unperturbed, and instructed Miss White to cobble something together and to go on a diet herself so that the paper could monitor her progress. Dutifully, though with the deepest reservations, she set about plundering a number of diet books she happened to have at home and produced a creditable introduction.

Let us just summarise the mess that Lloyd Turner's paper had got itself into. First it was paying for an advice column which its own staff was compiling; second, it was committed to paying Miss Dors thirteen instalments of £3,300 for a slimming programme that did not exist and was not exclusive.

In all this I do not think that Miss Dors can be blamed. If a newspaper is stupid enough to sign such a contract then she and her partner were only sensible to make the most of the opportunity. As one Daily Star employee involved in the affair said, 'They did nothing wrong. It was a fantastic coup.'

After the first part of the diet appeared, the paper employed, at further expense, a nutritionist who seems to have saved the situation somewhat by producing a programme which intelligibly instructed the reader how to lose weight without damaging his or her health. However, in the case of Miss White, still dieting on the instructions of her editor, it was not particularly successful: she gained between one and one and a half stones in weight during that summer. Meanwhile the Daily Star management tried to retrieve some of the money they were paying to Mr Waterfield's company by stopping a cheque. This measure does not appear to have been very successful either, since they failed to cancel the standing order which released £3,300 at regular intervals; the cheque was eventually re-issued.

You would have thought, perhaps, that the Daily Star would have learnt a lesson or two in the first six months of 1983, but this was not to be the case. Some time after the diet began to appear in the paper it was announced that Miss Dors was suffering from cancer, not I hasten to add in the Daily Star but in the News of the World. Lloyd Turner naturally felt that she and her problems were the property of the Daily Star and determined that his paper would be the first to photograph her recovering from treatment in hospital. Miss Dors obligingly agreed to this but added that a gesture of goodwill from the paper would not go amiss. He took the hint and generously offered her, her husband, Alan Lake, and their child a holiday to help them recuperate from the ordeal of the illness. When the paper, however, learnt that the family had booked for themselves a pleasant fortnight in a hotel in Tahiti the offer was promptly withdrawn.

The point of this extraordinary story, aside from demonstrating that agony columns and diet plans, like bingo games and horoscopes, are often not what they seem to be, is to show how a paper can lose all critical and commercial faculties in the cause of beating its rivals and promoting the glossiest, sexiest, light entertainment in town.

It would be disingenuous to express too much horror at the cynicism of popular newspaper editors, who are only behaving in the way we would expect. It is their cavalier behaviour that is so baffling.

CHAPTER 8

Pros and Cons

Not long ago, when the *Kensington News and West London Times* still circulated in the smarter suburbs of the capital, there began to appear in the columns of this distinguished local newspaper reports of a football team named Palmerston F.C. While most of the paper's sports pages were characterised by routine descriptions of untalented endeavour, the anonymous correspondent who followed Palmerston to its every fixture managed to file reports of such startling originality that they were invariably used. Other teams may have floundered in the mud for an hour and a half to produce goalless draws, but a Palmerston match rarely went by without some incredible feat, unheard of even in the First Division. Goals would be scored by Palmerston's goalkeeper, balls would perform fantastical tricks in the air and backs would achieve stupendous head-ins. The thrust of the Palmerston attack was constituted by the identical twins Mr C. and Mr D. Fairlie, neither of whom measured more than four foot ten in his football boots. Their reputation spread as far afield as Spain, where the legendary football manager Sordo Lopez (who coincidentally shared a name with an indifferent Spanish wine) resolved to sign them up. The result of his negotiations with Palmerston's team captain, John Marsden White, we shall never know, because the accounts of the games ceased as suddenly as they had begun. This was probably because Mr C. Fairlie (or was it Mr D.?) kicked a ball from the halfway line which, without leaving the turf, ended up in the net. This would have been a miraculous achievement for Pele, let alone an undersized centre-forward in local league football. In short the sports editor began to smell a rat. Eventually he discovered that he had been duped by a colleague on a neighbouring paper, the *Fulham Chronicle*. He resurrected Palmerston F.C. and sent them off on a tour of the Isle of Wight in which they scored two goals and conceded fifty. It was their last appearance in the paper, and nothing more was heard from the hoaxer.

Of course the poor fellow at the *Kensington News and West London Times* was a very easy target. Here was a man who, having endured the semi-literate effusions of minor team managers, was suddenly presented with readable, lively, well-expressed stories. Naturally he was not immediately going to doubt such a gift. For belief is frequently governed by expectation, and this tendency is especially well-developed in newspapermen, who in their longing for the world to be more exciting than it really is are willing to believe almost anything. An American lecturer in journalism, one Joe Skaggs, has been illustrating more or less this point for the last sixteen years. He variously presented himself to the American press as a scientist who had discovered a hormone produced by cockroaches that would cure nearly every illness, a gypsy leader who objected to the name of gypsy moth for America's tree pest and a windsurfer who planned to sail from Hawaii to the coast of California. In an interview given to the *National Enquirer*, perhaps the least reliable newspaper in the world, he was reported to have said, 'They'll rush into print with anything that smacks of a good yarn, hardly caring whether it's true or not. If a story is good they're not going to let it be ruined by facts. Every one of my hoaxes could have been exposed with one or two simple telephone calls.'

A wide range of impulses are present in the journalist's mind at any one time. Joachim Fest, writing in *Encounter* (November 1983), broadly defined them as being an overwhelming ambition to get into the limelight with a sensation; the spirit of journalistic competitiveness; a penchant for revealing secrets, for investigative reporting and even for mystery-mongering; and an eye for the news-stand sales.

These all appeared to a greater or lesser extent at Times Newspapers during the month of April 1983 when, on the fiftieth anniversary of Hitler's rise to power, Rupert Murdoch purchased the rights to his recently discovered diaries. It was the most significant and most shaming hoax to be practised on any newspaper for at least fifty years. What made it so bad was the fact that the original forgers, who had already bamboozled the West German magazine *Stern*, were motivated not by mischief or even commercial gain, but rather by a wish to rehabilitate Hitler, to endow him with thoughts and emotions to which we all could relate and to distance him from the ghastly crimes committed in his name.

Rumours of the diaries' existence first came to the attention of the *Sunday Times* before Murdoch had bought the paper from Lord Thomson. In 1980 Anthony Terry, then European Editor, had met Gerd Heidermann, a star reporter with the magazine *Stern* who told him that Hitler had dispatched a plane which carried all his personal documents from Berlin in the last days of the war. Previously it had been accepted that the plane had crashed en route from Berlin to Salzburg and that the archives had been destroyed. Heidermann's theory was that part of the material, including the Fuhrer's record of his rise and fall, had survived. Terry kept Heidermann's confidence except to relay the rumour to his newspaper. Nothing more was heard of Heidermann, and it was assumed by the *Sunday Times* that he had either been indulging in loose talk or had failed to locate the diaries. Two years later Magnus Linklater, one of the key executives on the paper, was approached by David Irving, the historian. Irving told him of a man named Professor August Presiack, who had knowledge of twenty-seven half-annual volumes of Hitler's diary. He offered to go to Germany on the paper's behalf to see if he could substantiate the rumours by getting a look at the 'silver-tooled volumes'. Acting on other academic advice, Linklater turned down the offer. These approaches, although not amounting to much, were important; they created in the minds of some *Sunday Times* journalists conditions under which they might accept the possibility of these diaries' existence.

On March 9, 1983, Peter Wickman, the London representative of *Stern*, contacted the *Sunday Times* and said his magazine was about to publish something of great historical importance. He would not divulge the nature of Stern's scoop until he had a written guarantee that the

Sunday Times would keep what he had to say secret. Having got the assurance he told the executives that in the middle of April *Stern* planned to publish the first instalments of the Diaries. He did not go into details about their whereabouts or their provenance. At first the *Sunday Times* was eager, but then it was pointed out that *Stern* published on a Thursday. How could the *Sunday Times* hope to keep such sensational material out of the British press until the following Sunday? The negotiations were therefore transferred over the bridge that connects the *Sunday Times* with its sister paper *The Times*. It was at this stage that Rupert Murdoch became interested.

Murdoch's intervention was to play an important part in the duping of his newspapers. For his commercial drive, his qualities as a negotiator and his eye for sensational publicity eventually ensured the humiliation of these two great newspapers. Another crucial factor in the events that followed was Wickman's insistence that the project and the negotiations should remain absolutely secret. No journalists below executive level, either on *The Times* or *Sunday Times*, were allowed to know about the discussions that were taking place, and therefore no one was in a position to counsel caution or insist on checks. The knowledge was restricted to Gerald Long, deputy chairman of News International, Frank Giles, editor of the *Sunday Times*, Brian MacArthur, his deputy, Charles Douglas-Home, editor of *The Times*, and Bruce Rothwell, an executive on Murdoch's *New York Post*. All were dominated by Murdoch's determination to clinch the deal with *Stern*. Those who witnessed his technique during the bargaining in *Stern*'s Hamburg headquarters came away mildly awed by his use of feigned indifference, enthusiasm, aggression and charm to get what he wanted. Although *Stern* was indubitably in the better position – Murdoch was competing with a rival interest from Sir David English at the *Daily Mail* – it was completely outwitted. *Stern* began by asking for 4.25 million dollars and insisted that the diaries would be released piecemeal. Murdoch concentrated his efforts on the figure rather than the condition, quickly bringing it down to 3.75 million dollars. At a critical point he withdrew from the haggling and let Bruce Rothwell give the impression that News International was losing interest. This did the trick and *Stern*, which had invested large amounts of money in Heidermann's story, began to worry that it would lose it. The magazine's representatives caved in and offered the British and American rights for 400,000 dollars, less than a tenth of the original figure. Murdoch's concern now was to steal the exclusive from *Stern* by beating them into print. This, to the eternal regret of journalists on *The Times* and *Sunday Times*, he managed with consummate ease.

During the weeks of frenetic negotiating an approximation of what Murdoch was up to began to circulate in Gray's Inn Road. Frank Giles alerted Eric Jacobs, the Review-front editor, that the diaries were in the offing and that he might have to clear his pages at very short notice. Jacobs then told his friend and colleague Philip Knightley, a leading investigative reporter. On April 20, five days after he had talked to Jacobs, Knightley sent a note to Giles which made great play of the similarities between the Hitler Diaries and the Mussolini Diaries, which had been bought by the paper for £250,000 in the sixties. The memorandum was, perhaps, the first sensible consideration that anyone on either of the papers had given to the dangers involved:

1) You cannot rely on expert authentication. Thompson engaged five experts, including the author of the standard work on Mussolini, the world's greatest authority on paper, a famous handwriting expert, an internationally known paleographer and an academic who authenticated the Casement Diaries. NOT ONE EXPERT SAID THAT THEY WERE FAKE.

2) You cannot rely on people close to the subject. Vittorio Mussolini, Mussolini's son, said that the diaries were definitely his father's.

3) You cannot rely on legal protection. Slaughter and May [a firm of solicitors] did the negotiations for Thomson. They did not succeed in recovering a single penny when the diaries turned out to be fakes.

4) Beware of secrecy and being pressed to make a quick decision. The Mussolini con-men were able to bring off their sting by pressing Thompson to make a quick deal. Absolute secrecy was essential, they said, to prevent the Italian government

from stepping in. Both manoeuvres prevented proper examination of the background of the salesmen and the provenance of the diaries.

QUESTIONS TO CONSIDER.

1) What German academic experts have seen all the diaries. Has, for instance the Institute of Contemporary History seen them?

2) What non-academic British experts have seen all the diaries? Has David Irving seen them?

3) How thoroughly has the vendor explained where the diaries have been all these years and why have they surfaced NOW; the fiftieth anniversary of Hitler's accession to power!

The crux of the matter is that secrecy and speed work for the con-man. To mount a proper check would protect us but would not be acceptable to the vendor. Nevertheless, WE SHOULD INSIST ON DOING OUR OWN CHECKS and not accept the checks of any other publishing organisation.

This was a rather remarkable piece of insight. For, although Knightley had not the slightest idea about the conditions and terms of the sale, he had pinpointed exactly the reasons why Murdoch and his editors should have been moving with caution. For obsessive secrecy and the desire for speed had been at the heart of *Stern*'s behaviour in the past six weeks. However, he might as well not have written the memo for all the good it did. He recalls Giles's reaction when they bumped into each other in the lavatory: 'He said that the whole thing had been authenticated by Lord Dacre and that anyway it wasn't his worry since the diaries were likely to be serialised in *The Times* and not the *Sunday Times*.' This did seem to be at variance with what Giles had told Jacobs, but Knightley ignored the inconsistency and began to ponder the role of Lord Dacre.

It is often a sign of journalists' inner weakness and the lack of conviction in their own judgment that they place so much trust in academics. The general attitude to Lord Dacre, an expert in the period, an independent director of *The Times* and, as it happens, a relation of Charles Douglas-Home, was little short of reverential. When he emerged from the Swiss bank vault where the Diaries were kept and declared that he was quite confident that they were not a fake, everyone accepted his word. Others had seen them too. Bruce Rothwell remarked that they 'gave off good vibes' and Douglas-Home, author of Rommel's biography, delivered himself of the opinion that they 'smelt old and musty'. Much like the sports editor of the *Kensington News and West London Times* they all believed what they wanted to believe. The 'musty smell' and the 'good vibes' were simply wish-fulfilment.

Things were relatively relaxed at the *Sunday Times* until Friday, April 22, when Frank Giles summoned Magnus Linklater and Hugo Young, the political editor, and informed them that, contrary to what he had told Knightley, the *Sunday Times* would be devoting a substantial part of the next issue to the diaries. Young and Linklater, who have both since left the paper, exploded, saying that it was irresponsible to run such a sensational story in the paper when it was untried and unchecked by the *Sunday Times* journalists. Linklater says now, 'We spent the whole day trying to dissuade Frank, but he was adamant. He said it was a major deal and there was absolutely no point in arguing even though he agreed that the situation was far from satisfactory in journalistic terms.'

That day Knightley, accompanied by Gitta Sereny, the reporter who had followed up many of the early hints the paper had received, attended the annual press awards lunch where they encountered the editor of the *Times*. 'He was behaving with a remarkable insouciance,' Knightly said. 'Although I and Gitta did not know at the time that the *Sunday Times* was publishing the diaries, he did.' On his return to the office Knightley rang Lord Dacre to talk to him about the authentication process. He put this question to the venerable historian: 'Isn't it rather curious that these should appear on the fiftieth anniversary of Hitler's accession to power? Is there a Nazi plot to rehabilitate Hitler's reputation?' Dacre thought for a moment and replied, 'I haven't really thought about that . . . ' Knightley was convinced by Dacre's certainty; however, the conversation seems to have preyed on the academic's mind and as we shall see the reporter's insistent questioning was to have considerable consequence the next day.

Knightley might have been persuaded, but Linklater and Paul Eddy, the former editor of Insight, who was now deeply involved in putting together the Hitler Diaries coverage, still had their doubts. 'We knew,' said Linklater, 'that we faced a decision; either we should refuse to take part in the exercise and resign or we should have to bite the bullet and get on with it. Both of us now recognise that we should have done the honourable thing but instead we got on with it. Once we had taken that decision the whole thing became rather fun.'

This last remark is crucial. Linklater, although as intelligent and as sceptical a journalist as you are likely to find, abandoned his better judgment and allowed himself to be swept along by the excitement generated by Murdoch's purchase. While they prepared for Sunday, *The Times* went to bed with the following story. Under the headline HITLER SECRET DIARIES TO BE PUBLISHED, Michael Binyon wrote:

> Sixty volumes of hitherto unknown diaries kept by Adolf Hitler throughout his twelve-year dictatorship have been discovered after lying for almost 35 years concealed at an undisclosed location in East Germany.
>
> The documents are of momentous historic significance. They are now in a Swiss bank vault and have been painstakingly tested and analysed by experts, including handwriting analysts from the Federal Archives in Koblenz, for the past two years. Lord Dacre, who as Mr Hugh Trevor-Roper investigated the circumstances of Hitler's death for British intelligence after the war, is among those who are convinced that the diaries are genuine.
>
> Extracts from the astonishing documents, which will significantly alter historical judgments on Hitler's strategic thinking, exercise of power and personality, are to be published in West Germany by the weekly magazine *Stern*. They are also to be serialised in the *Sunday Times*.

Lord Dacre was quoted as saying:

> 'When I entered the back room in the Swiss bank and turned the pages of those volumes, and learnt the extraordinary story of their discovery, my doubts gradually dissolved away.
>
> 'I am now satisfied that the documents are authentic and that

the standard accounts of Hitler's writing habits, of his personality
and even, perhaps, of some public events may, in consequence,
have to be revised.'

The next morning, Saturday, Lord Dacre woke up feeling rather less
confident than he had the previous day. He read *The Times* and resolved
to ring Charles Douglas-Home to express his worries. He made the call
at 8.00 a.m., some eleven hours before the first edition of the *Sunday
Times* was due to carry the first excerpts to the nation. Dacre was quite
definite; he had changed his mind overnight and he felt *The Times* ought
to know. Even at this distance in time it still seems incredible that
Douglas-Home informed neither Frank Giles, at the *Sunday Times*, nor
any other Murdoch employee of Dacre's recantation. Karen Rothmyer
of the *Columbia Journalism Review* thought that this was the most
interesting part of the whole Hitler Diaries débâcle. She first asked
Dacre why he had not told the *Sunday Times*. He replied, 'I had no
dealings with them. I had been employed solely by *The Times*.' She
moved on to ask Douglas-Home why he had not alerted Frank Giles.
He said that he thought Dacre would have expressed any doubts he had
to Knightley. After that he declined to make any further comment.

His silence during these eleven hours was curious in the extreme and
has still not been explained. It was, after all, within his power for the
whole of that day to prevent Frank Giles and the staff of the *Sunday
Times* from printing what turned out to be an obvious fraud, cobbled
together by a con-man in his spare time. And yet he did nothing.

In the event Frank Giles and his senior journalists were to find out
about Dacre's doubts that evening just as the first edition was being
despatched to the furthest corners of the British Isles. They had
assembled in the editor's office for a small celebration drink. As a
matter of form, Giles decided to ring Dacre to let him know that all was
well and that four pages of the paper were devoted to the diaries.
Linklater was there. 'We were all talking but gradually each one of us
shut up as we caught words from Frank's conversation. The room was
completely silent by the time Frank said, "Now come on Hugh, don't
tell me you're having doubts now. I trust you are not making a 180-
degree turn . . . oh, you are."'

It is important in all this to recognise that while the *Times* editor had done little to help his colleagues, they had done little to help themselves. Although they all had their separate doubts, there was, in their behaviour, a remarkable passivity, a fatalistic acceptance of the dubious information that their enthusiastic proprietor had foisted on them.

What, then, was the material that had caused Rupert Murdoch to deploy every trick he had learnt as an international publisher, Lord Dacre to abandon all academic standards and the journalists of the paper to surrender their professional scepticism? Well, when it comes down to it such extracts that the paper published were remarkably unconvincing. They were thin on historical detail, provided no insight into the personality of the supposed author and were peppered with pointless and banal observations. From the very first excerpt, printed in Brian MacArthur's trailer on the front page, it was quite clear that the diary was fake:

November 19, 1932: From now on I shall keep my political actions and thoughts in notes in order to preserve them for posterity like every other politician.

Does this sound genuine? Is this the sort of resolution that Hitler would commit in such simple terms to his new diary? No, of course not. The sentence was intended to be read by some future purchaser such as Gerd Heidermann. MacArthur's story continued:

As the diary grew, those thoughts, now published for the first time in the *Sunday Times*, ranged across the emotions. There was the commonplace 'suffering more and more from insomnia; indigestion getting worse' (April 1938); the deadly, 'I also don't need any kind of investigations by Himmler. He is also snooping on Eva' (April 1935); the worldly, 'The English are worrying me. Shall I let them go or not? How will Churchill react?' (May 20, 1940, Dunkirk).

He also developed a grudging respect for Neville Chamberlain on the day after Britain, France and Italy agreed to hand over parts of Czechoslovakia to Germany. Hitler wrote on September 30, 1938, 'He nearly outsmarted me this smoothie Englishman ... I would have made quite different conditions for Mussolini and Daladier, but I couldn't do so with this cunning fox Chamberlain.

My favourite extracts are when Hitler turns his thoughts to the German leadership:

> That little Dr Goebbels is up to his old tricks again with women. I shall issue a secret instruction that I do not wish to have any more of these love affairs by my closest associates and the Party leaders in the Reich.

And

> I shall show this deceitful small animal breeder [Himmler] with his lust for power; this unfathomable little penny pincher will find out what I am really like.

And

> Bormann wants me to give him all my documents. He is going to pack them in containers and send them off. This Bormann has been indispensible to me. If I had five Bormanns I would not have been sitting here now.

This was one of the last entries and, like the first, was written to convince. While everyone at the *Sunday Times* may have suspended their disbelief, the rest of Fleet Street lost no time in heaping scorn on the paper's World Exclusive. The following day the world's press assembled in Hamburg for the official launch of *Stern*'s serialisation. The editor-in-chief, Peter Koch, had naturally invited Lord Dacre, whose support appeared to remain as firm as ever (none of his doubts had been carried in the *Sunday Times*). The evening before Lord Dacre had had a chance to talk to Gerd Heidermann and ask the questions that he should perhaps have put before. Heidermann gave him no satisfaction, particularly in the all-important area of where he had acquired the diaries.

One can hardly imagine a less successful press launch. Instead of adding his weight to the serialisation, Dacre announced that he could no longer guarantee the authenticity of the diaries. The *Daily Mail* captured the Dacre volte-face in two quotes which it ran in bold type on its centre spread:

QUESTION: Lord Dacre, do you still believe the so-called Hitler Diaries to be genuine?

ANSWER: I was misled . . . the thing looks more shaky . . . they may be real but there is such a thing as a perfect forgery.

Later in the wonderfully amusing colour piece by Brian Jones, Lord Dacre was quoted as saying:

The whole question of the authenticity of the diaries is inseparable from the history of the diaries. We have evidence that important documents from Hitler were on board that destroyed aircraft. Are these documents before us necessarily linked to the aeroplane?

'When I saw these documents in Zurich I understood – perhaps misunderstood – that the link was absolutely established, that one man had been responsible for securing the documents in 1945 and that the same man today has vouched for them. But now I understand it is not as I had thought.'

If one reads the *Sunday Times* stories today, it is possible to detect the odd note of caution and the occasional qualification woven into the boastful Exclusive. But after Dacre's defection in Hamburg, Fleet Street saw no need to concede this. Auberon Waugh, who is unequalled in the field of wounding abuse, wrote in the *Spectator*:

The whole story stinks from beginning to end. Why did the Editors of the *Times* and *Sunday Times* touch this rubbish, let alone Lord Dacre? Presumably the Editor of the *Sunday Times* hopes to add to his miserable readership of half-wits and illiterates.

The other Sunday newspapers had long been irritated by the *Sunday Times*'s style and self-importance, not to mention quality. The *Observer* and the *Mail on Sunday* (the *Sunday Times*'s chief commercial rivals) both thought it would be amusing to begin their investigations by aping the Len Deighton-thriller style that the *Sunday Times* often uses to introduce stories of great moment. The *Observer* team wrote:

It was first edition time at the *Sunday Times*.

Or (as the paper's own writers like to put these things) it was

5.29 pm on Saturday, 23 April. At New Printing House Square
the ink was wet and the presses were ready to roll. A light drizzle
was falling outside. Insistently, a telephone was ringing.

And the *Mail on Sunday*:

Just after five o'clock last Saturday Brian MacArthur, the
chubby, likable deputy editor of the *Sunday Times*, strolled around
the paper's newsroom on the fifth floor of its offices in Gray's Inn
Road.

There was a broad smile on his face and a proof of the next
day's front page in his hand.

'Look at that,' he said proudly to some of the younger reporters,
'you will never see another front page like that as long as you live.
It is sensational.'

For its own part, the *Sunday Times* devoted rather less space to the
Hitler Diaries than it had the previous week, and, of course, the
promised extracts did not appear. Instead the paper announced that
the serialisation was still planned for May, 'unless, on the balance of
probability, they are shown not to be authentic.' It was a question of
proof which the *Sunday Times* found impossible to elicit from the
vendors. Any number of experts were consulted by the press but all they
had to offer was opinion.

David Irving, who at the time just happened to be publishing his
biography of Hitler's doctor, was one who was very much in evidence.
His role was a curious one; having enthusiastically urged the *Sunday
Times* to follow up the first rumours in the winter, he lost no time in
denouncing them at the Hamburg press conference and for his pains
got much coverage for his biography of Dr Theodore Morell. But just
when it was clear that the diaries were a crude fake, Irving issued a
statement to the effect that he had had a meeting with *Stern* representatives and that in view of his own discoveries about Hitler's Parkinson's
disease, he was inclined to believe that the diaries were the genuine
article. Needless to say this won Irving a great deal more publicity,
though it did not help the cause for truth.

The denouement came on the following Friday when Hans Booms,
the president of the General Federal Archives in Koblenz, announced

that his analysis of the glue, binding and thread used in one of the volumes proved that they were all of post-war material and manufacture. His colleagues had also examined the text and found that it was based on a compilation of Hitler's speeches and proclamations.

Meanwhile *Stern*, on the insistence of Murdoch, had delivered another volume to the *Sunday Times* which was duly conveyed to a forensic expert, Dr Julius Grant. He took no time at all to establish that the papers contained a chemical which only came into use after the war. Had *Stern* and Murdoch insisted on such tests before announcing the discovery and making international asses of themselves, the story would have been very different indeed.

Secrecy and speed were the things that Philip Knightley had warned of. It was *Stern*'s obsessive secrecy and Rupert Murdoch's excessive haste that caused the humiliations of the *Sunday Times* and, we must not forget, *The Times*.

On May 8 it fell to poor Brian MacArthur to explain the paper's rash behaviour to *Sunday Times* readers. It was a difficult piece to write, since he had at all costs to maintain the paper's dignity as well as apologise for the ineffable stupidity of its management. He started with a phrase which was to become the subject of much hilarity from the rivals who had so enjoyed the paper's downfall:

Serious journalism is a high-risk business. Not for the first time, the *Sunday Times* took a high risk by its own involvement with the so-called Hitler Diaries. For the first time, very regrettably, the risk proved to be a mistake. [MacArthur appears to have forgotten the Mussolini Diaries.] We owe our readers a sincere apology.

By our own lights we did not act irresponsibly. When major but hazardous stories seem to be appearing, a newspaper can either dismiss them without enquiry or pursue investigations to see if they are true.

Above MacArthur's apology (or apologia) Gitta Sereny and Philip Knightley, the two main sceptics at the *Sunday Times*, wrote stories about Heidermann and the as-yet unnamed forger. If Sereny had been allowed to play a greater part in the events of a month before, it is possible that the paper would not have given such public credence to the discovery.

On the fateful Saturday when Douglas-Home failed to telephone Frank Giles she, although maintaining an open mind in the matter, decided to see if the diaries had been submitted to the rigorous tests claimed by *Stern*. After one or two telephone calls she established that no one at the Federal Archives 'had heard of, much less seen, any diaries'. What they had been given by *Stern* were some Hitler documents and a few blank pages cut from one of the volumes. She informed various executives of her discovery. They took no notice, which seems to me to indicate that aside from the factors of speed and secrecy there was a good element of what Joe Skaggs, the American media hoaxer, described as the wish to print anything that smacks of a 'good yarn', whether it is true or not.

She was to spend the next seven months unravelling how the forgery came about and how Gerd Heidermann had first been duped and then implicated in it. Her story, published in the *Sunday Times* in December 1983, was a disturbing one not just because it showed how easily great newspapers and magazines had been conned but also because it proved that veterans of the Third Reich had used the Diaries to prettify Hitler. The trial began with one Konrad Kujau, who had confessed to the West German police that he was the forger. He was unabashed by Sereny's questioning and willingly showed how he could write in Hitler's handwriting at dictation speed.

He estimated that such was his mastery of Hitler's hand and his knowledge of the history of the Third Reich that it took him as little as two and a half hours to compose one of the sixty volumes. A lesser reporter would not have bothered to go any deeper. After all, she had established the link between Heidermann and Kujau. All that seemed necessary was to divine their motives, determine where the *Stern*'s £2,500,000 had disappeared to and write up the interviews with the broker Heidermann and the bumptious clown Kujau. But with an acute eye for inconsistencies Sereny spotted that Kujau, despite his boasting, was not capable of masterminding the forgery on his own. She also noted that his conversation was full of lies, particularly in relation to the date when he is supposed to have started work on the diaries. Kujau, for instance, said that he had begun in the late 1970s, when Sereny knew that an unbound volume from his pen had been offered for sale in America as early as 1976. These early efforts, it turned out, were simply forged for commercial reasons. It became obvious to Sereny that at some stage, presumably when there was an established market for the diaries, somebody had begun to make strong suggestions as to the contents of the diaries.

She found the answer to the problem in the recent life of Heidermann who, as one of the credulous, impressionable personalities that newspapers occasionally attract, had become involved on the periphery of a number of ex-Nazi organisations. His own fascination for the Hitler era had led him to buy Herman Goering's yacht *Coria II* and restore it. This was the entrée to other collectors of the artefacts of fascism. One of them turned out to be supplied by Kujau who, using the name Konrad Fischer, worked as a dealer. Quite by chance Heidermann learnt that 'Fischer' had a source in East Germany who had access to some of Hitler's diaries. He tried to contact 'Fischer' with a view to buying the diaries for *Stern*, but failed. Early in 1980 Heidermann met a sinister figure named Medard Klapper, a member of ex-S.S. associations and a former member of the Hitler bodyguard.

Sereny's thesis, which seems probable, was that Klapper effected the introduction between Heidermann and Kujau with the intention of relieving *Stern* of considerable amounts of money and displaying the acceptable face of the Führer. Klapper also told Heidermann that Martin Bormann was alive and living in Spain. Once the diaries began to emerge from Kujau's workshop Klapper arranged for them to be 'verified' by Bormann. In the light of Kujau's revelation that Heidermann discovered about the forgery in 1981, one must wonder why he continued to insist on Bormann's existence. Nevertheless he did, perhaps because, as I have said before, he wanted to believe it. Meanwhile Klapper actively started collecting real information from a source in West Germany's state archives. This, Sereny believed, was presented to Kujau who subsequently incorporated it in the text of the diaries.

Klapper denied his part in the hoax and when Sereny interviewed him went on insisting that Martin Bormann was still alive and, furthermore, that he would introduce her to him (this has not yet happened). Klapper's denial is particularly untrustworthy since Sereny proved that he received upwards of £46,000 from the bank-account that *Stern* had set up to finance Heidermann's investigations.

As the generous contributor to the ex-Nazi organisation, HIAG, Klapper had every reason to further the forger's work. More important, he used the opportunity to create the harmless, human Hitler of the diaries.

Thus Times Newspapers became the instrument of an exceedingly unpleasant S.S. officer. The hoax might have come off if Heidermann and Kujau had constructed a more convincing provenance and had taken the trouble to use materials from the period. Still, considering their inadequacies, they got quite far enough on the credulity of British and German journalists.

Times Newspapers lost nothing financially; none of *Stern*'s fee was paid and the *Sunday Times*'s circulation jumped by 60,000 copies. What the organisation did lose, however, was more serious: it destroyed the credibility of the *Sunday Times*, built up over a fifteen-year period in which it had become one of the world's most trusted and admired newspapers.

CHAPTER 9

The Press Council
We Deserve

'I do not hate the Press Council. I just think they are a pussy-footing arm of the establishment,' Harold Evans reports Rupert Murdoch as saying.

One of the more eccentric acts of the editor of Murdoch's *Sunday Times*, Frank Giles, during the Hitler Diaries fiasco was to run an editorial comment ticking off the Press Council. If ever there was a case of someone beholding the mote in his brother's eye while failing to consider the whopping great beam in his own, then this was it. Still, Mr Giles's leader made a rather good point: that it was extremely unsatisfactory of the Press Council, which stood for openness and free discussion, to conduct its own affairs, particularly the appointment of Sir Patrick Neill's successor as chairman, with the sort of secrecy one finds in Whitehall. The article maintained that an open discussion of the issues involved was the only way to persuade Parliament that the Press Council was a true guardian of the public interest and, more important, that the newspaper industry was perfectly capable of regulating itself without legislation. Since it was founded in 1953, the main objective of the Press Council has been to preserve the established freedom of the press, which is generally thought to be done best by resisting all Parliament's legislative ambitions. So far politicians have been persuaded that other elements of the Council's constitution see to it that the press is properly controlled. As summarised in Geoffrey Robertson's excellent study of the Council, *People Against The Press* (Quartet, 1983), they are:

To maintain the character of the British Press in accordance with the highest professional and commercial standards.

To consider complaints about the conduct of the press or the conduct of persons and organisations toward the press; to deal with these complaints in whatever manner might seem practical and appropriate and record resultant action.

To keep under review developments likely to restrict the supply of information of public interest and importance.

To report publicly on developments that may lead towards concentration or monopoly in the press (including changes in ownership, control and growth of press undertakings) and to publish statistical information relating thereto.

To make representations on appropriate occasions to the government, organs of the United Nations and the press organisations abroad.

To publish periodical reports recording the Council's work and to review from time to time developments in the press and factors affecting them.

The main work of the Council is the consideration of complaints from the public on the contents of newspapers. In this it is supposed to operate on the lines of something like the Advertising Standards Authority, which ensures legality, decency and honesty in commercials. However, as we have seen, the Press Council is less than successful in controlling the excesses of Fleet Street.

Most of its funding (all but £10,000 of an annual income of £478,000) comes from various groups of newspaper proprietors. The Council is run by eleven full-time staff including the director, Ken Morgan, and the assistant director, Charles White. There are thirty-six members of the Council itself, half of which are nominated by the newspaper industry while the other half are selected by an Appointments Commission. At the top is part-time chairman Sir Zelman Cowen Q.C.

While the director may occasionally pronounce on issues of editorial freedom, as in the dispute between the editor of the *Observer*, Donald Trelford, and his proprietor, Tiny Rowland, or of journalists' rights, as in the case of the *New Statesman* journalist Duncan Campbell, whose home was searched by police, or of the general standards of the press, as in Fleet Street's obsession with bingo, it is the success or otherwise of the Council's work in the area of complaints on which its entire credibility must lie. For if it is perceived that the Council is unable to give complainants satisfaction where they deserve it, people are hardly going to take notice of its views, however justified and reasonable they might be. On the face of it the business of receiving complaints, deciding whether they should be investigated and adjudicating on matters of fact, taste and fairness does not seem to be very complicated. After all, it is more or less the process that is carried out in every court in the land with relative ease. However, the Council's work in 1983 suggests otherwise.

Robertson has identified several areas in which the complainant is placed at a distinct disadvantage by the procedures of the Council. For one thing, unlike the libel laws, the burden of proof is placed on the complainant. He or she is first required to produce sufficient evidence for the Council to consider the complaint and then further evidence and argument during the hearing. Moreover, while newspaper editors are given the opportunity of an oral hearing, the complainant is not. Finally, the complainant is required to waive his or her legal rights; that is to say he or she may not sue for libel following a Press Council judgment. Although the last is obviously an infringement on the individual's right of access to the courts, it has not been tested by law and complainants in the Council's thirty-one-year history have all had to accept this irksome condition.

Suppose, therefore, that a popular newspaper were to describe me as a 'glue-sniffing Trotskyite' and I felt that this ought to be corrected in some way. My choice is either the law courts or the Press Council. In this case I decide that I am more interested in a correction of fact than in claiming damages, my decision no doubt influenced by the fact that a deposit of £10,000 is usually required even to start a libel action. So I write to the Council with my complaint. The Council agrees to take it up, but before doing so tells me that I will have no further redress and, furthermore, that I will be expected to provide proof that I am not a glue-sniffing Trotskyite. This may be obvious, but it is not always easy to supply proof of the self-evident. When the Council comes to consider the dreadful slur on my character, I discover not only that the editor of the paper concerned has opted to address the Council personally, but also that his newspaper is represented by a silken-tongued lawyer, which I, as the complainant, am not allowed. Is it any wonder that so many complaints are abandoned before they reach this stage?

One of the chief problems of the Press Council is that only a very small percentage of the population know of its existence and their right to apply to it. Consider the *Sun*'s World Exclusive interview with the wife of Sergeant McKay. Here was an obvious case for the Press Council and yet, presumably because she was not aware of what the Council did or how to approach it, Mrs McKay did not consider an application. It was Caroline Metcalfe, secretary to the *Observer*'s diarist, Peter Hillmore, who complained. The reaction of the Press Council defies understanding. The assistant director, Charles White, replied to Mrs Metcalfe with a letter that was clearly designed to deter her:

> I would ask you to bear in mind that a complaints committee would be no better placed than yourself to assess the truth of two conflicting newspaper stories unless it is provided with independent evidence supporting one version. If you wish to pursue a complaint, would you be able to provide such informa-tion for the complaints committee?

Eventually the case was heard and the Press Council produced its adjudication. Two things ought to be said about this. First, the language the Council used to censure this, one of the worst cases of newspaper deceit it is possible to imagine, was inadequate and in no way expressed the outrage that was necessary. Second, the adjudication was released on August 8, some eight months after the Council had received Mrs Metcalfe's letter.

One often senses in reading these judgments a real lack of convic-tion, a wish not to offend the culpable publication too much. Certainly this timorous approach displayed itself in the Council's behaviour towards Peter Tatchell, who, although most newspapers did not think so, had as much right to redress as any other citizen who has been abused by journalists. Tatchell records in his book that he made eight separate complaints to the Council about press distortion. The Council acknowledged the letters of Tatchell's press officer, Peter Robinson, the actual complainant, and waited.

They received no further letters from Robinson which was regrettable but quite understandable during a by-election, especially if Robinson was confronted with the sort of off-putting, pettifogging nonsense displayed in Charles White's letter to Mrs Metcalfe. Surely Press Council members observed that Tatchell was getting less than fair treatment in the press? Having received an initial approach, the Council should have made it easy for Mr Tatchell to outline his complaints. The Press Council, when rightly criticised by Tatchell's book, replied that it had sent many letters that went unanswered.

One wonders why on earth Ken Morgan or Charles White did not telephone the Bermondsey Labour Party office. Even had they actually managed to reach the stage of agreeing on the terms of complaint, it seems doubtful whether the Press Council would have been any use in correcting some of the appalling publicity Tatchell received before polling day. As it was, the Council's only public pronouncement on the Tatchell affair was a short and rather petulant press release which appeared on publication of *The Battle For Bermondsey*, which indicated to me at least that the Council was a good deal more anxious about its image than about the undoubted wrongs perpetrated against the candidate.

The delays involved in the Press Council's cumbersome procedure are the chief reason why complaints are abandoned. Robert Hughes, the Labour M.P., had to wait eight months before the Council censured the *Daily Express* for a thoroughly inaccurate and damaging report during the General Election. And Mrs Daphne Francis, who complained about the reporting of Michael Heseltine's visit to Newbury, was kept waiting for ten months. Occasionally the Council can act quickly, as it did when the Labour party complained about the *Daily Mail*'s story that Nissan would not build a car plant in Britain if the party won the election. But this only goes to demonstrate that there is a

vast difference between the Council's reaction to an individual complaint and to the grievance of a powerful, well-organised body like the
Labour party. In my view there was just as much urgency to settle
Tatchell's complaints in a by-election as there was to deal speedily with
the *Daily Mail*'s story in a General Election.

In recognition of this criticism, the Council has started what it calls a
'fast-track' service, designed to achieve a quick correction of factual
errors, or a quick ruling where complainants and editors cannot agree.
Under this system the complainant must make his request to the editor
for a correction within three days of an inaccuracy appearing and tell
the Press Council that he has done so. The editor then has three days in
which to correct the inaccuracy or tell the complainant he is not doing
so.

In disputed cases the complainant should tell the Press Council
within two further days and a panel, consisting of two Press Council
members and the director, will rule within the next three days. The
'fast-track' is only open to people and organisations complaining about
significant factual inaccuracies in stories that name or identify them
clearly. This is certainly an improvement, and one hopes it is used well.
However, the Council has done little to publicise its new service and
one suspects that the general ignorance means that the national press
will still get away with a lot.

The introduction of the 'fast-track' service was due in no small
measure to the growing demand for a statutory right of reply. When
Labour M.P. Frank Allaun introduced his Right of Reply Bill into
Parliament it attracted support from both sides of the house and came
within a whisker of reaching the Second Reading stage in the spring of
1983. The idea that the right of reply may become law in the near future
horrifies anyone who is connected with the press. Robertson explains
what the bill, as drafted by Allaun, would have meant:

> The Allaun Bill would give a right of reply by obliging
> newspapers, on pain of a £40,000 fine, to publish counter-
> statements by companies and organisations of equal length to
> reports which are alleged to be 'distorted'. Thus no editor could
> give substantial space to investigative reporting or campaigning

journalism about business or politics without the prospect of
providing equal space for an extended reply.

The effects of the Allaun Bill would of course be ludicrous; a good third
of the newspapers each day might be given over to replies which would
not themselves necessarily be accurate. The Press Council expressed
its anxiety thus: 'Part of the Council's concern about the Right of Reply
Bill is its failure to distinguish between inaccuracies and distortion: the
one relatively easy to identify, the other sometimes intensely arguable.
The Bill does not distinguish between material originated by a
newspaper itself and inaccuracies or criticism which it merely reports,
for example attacks upon on one politician by another.'

Of course, many of the inadequacies of Allaun's proposal would have
been removed during its progress through the various stages of
legislation; however one can imagine the sort of ill-conceived and
vengeful bill the Labour party might rush through Parliament on its
return to power. Ken Morgan, himself a journalist, sees it as the Press
Council's most pressing duty to counter the right of reply argument
whenever it comes up: 'So far, we in Britain have believed it would be
tampering with freedom too much. We have preferred to rely on
voluntary restrictions and voluntary machinery. However, if it subsequently proves that editors are being less than candid, they play into
the hands of those who want a statutory authority, a ministry in charge
of the press even.'

Unfortunately, anyone arguing in favour of legislation was presented
in 1983 with a fine example of the impotence of the Council and all its
voluntary restrictions and machinery. In February the Press Council
published the results of its long enquiry into the conduct of the press
following the arrest and conviction of the Yorkshire Ripper, Peter
Sutcliffe. It proved that four national newspapers had not only
attempted to deceive the public as to payments it was making to
Sutcliffe's relatives, but had also consistently refused to help the
Council in its investigations. Much of the important information
received by the Council came into its possession quite by chance from
Mrs Sonia Sutcliffe, who had kept all the model contracts, the letters
and the scraps of paper that had been posted through her letterbox.

With the approval of her solicitor she sent the entire file to the Council. It was very illuminating indeed, particularly in regard to the *Daily Mail*, which had presented itself in editorials as a fine, upstanding newspaper that would never dream of negotiating contracts with the relatives of a mass murderer. What the *Mail* did not tell its readership was that it had negotiated a contract of £5,000 with John Sutcliffe, Peter's father, entertained members of the family at a hotel and, worse still, persistently offered large amounts of money to the killer's wife. The recently knighted David English told the Council that within days of Peter Sutcliffe's arrest he had come to a decision that it would be wrong to pay money to Mrs Sutcliffe because *Daily Mail* readers would be deeply offended. Later he protested to the Council that newspapers were entitled on the grounds of public interest to talk to Mrs Sutcliffe and, if necessary, pay her for her interview.

The file from Mrs Sutcliffe's solicitor proved, or at least seemed to prove, that he had all along believed the latter statement. For it contained a draft contract with an accompanying letter from the *Daily Mail*. The letter said that, 'the negotiations could also include the possibility of making some kind of provision for the other families who have suffered.' Sir David English's explanation when confronted with this was that his paper used the offer of money to build up a relationship with Mrs Sutcliffe and to spoil other newspapers' negotiations. He admitted that the *Daily Mail* had done this with the intention of deceiving Mrs Sutcliffe and her solicitor. The Press Council obviously wondered if it was not being deceived too. In the adjudications it admitted: 'It has been difficult for the Press Council to determine whether some of the incidents in the story it has been told were merely ploys intended to convey to Mrs Sutcliffe the false impression that she might be paid for her story or were genuine proposals to pay her.' In the end it decided to accept the word of four editorial executives that they knew of the editor's decision that the *Daily Mail* should not pay her. I wonder if they were right. Within six months the Council found itself again addressing the subject of the *Daily Mail*'s relations with Mrs Sutcliffe. Following stories in *Private Eye* and a commendable programme by Granada's *World in Action* team, the Council found that the

Daily Mail had failed to disclose that a further £3,000 worth of hospitality had been given to the Sutcliffe family. Considering the amounts being talked about, £3,000 was a negligible sum. But the fact remains that the paper had dissembled to its readers in the account of its behaviour and had deceived the Press Council. If it was prepared to deceive on this small matter one wonders how much trust we can place in the assurances that the *Mail* had no intention of paying Mrs Sutcliffe. The *News of the World*, too, had failed to disclose precisely the extent of its activities. From the date of Sutcliffe's arrest to the spring of 1981 the paper made persistent efforts to lure his wife into a contract. The negotiations culminated in an offer of no less than £110,000 which was posted along with a contract and an assurance that the story would be treated with the utmost compassion. Aside from the fact that the *News of the World* also hid the extent of its offers, the most interesting part of the Council's inquiry was the response of Henry Douglas, the paper's legal manager and, I am amazed to discover, a member of the Press Council until 1980. He opined that it was wrong of Mrs Sutcliffe to release all this damaging evidence against the *News of the World*: 'Letters written to lawyers and through him [Douglas] to her should not have been disclosed to a third party, the Press Council.'

It goes without saying that this is a pretty strange view, coming as it does from somebody who presumably believes that for their own sake newspapers should be utterly candid in their dealings with the Council.

Like the *Daily Mail* and the *News of the World*, the *Daily Express* maintained to the Council that no money had been offered to Mrs Sutcliffe. Her solicitor's file proved otherwise. A few days after Sutcliffe's arrest the *Daily Express* had, together with another paper, offered her £50,000. This was followed up by an offer of £80,000 and a letter from the editor saying he would be happy to discuss any arrangements she would wish to make. In a written reply to the Council, the editor said that he had forgotten about these offers.

The most hypocritical of all editors was Mr Lloyd Turner of the *Daily Star*. His paper had been censured in the general report on press conduct for breaking the Council's Declaration of Principle which forbids newspapers from making payment to potential witnesses. The

Star had paid £4,000 to Olivia Reivers, who was with Sutcliffe when he was arrested and thus was almost certain to be called to give evidence. In a show of penitence Lloyd Turner said that he agreed with the Council's decision to extend its Declaration of Principle to bar newspaper payments to the associates and family of a criminal. The Council reported:

> One newspaper which took a leading part in the discussion with the Press Council of the desirability of extending the Declaration to prevent the relatives of a criminal receiving payments made on the back of crime, was the *Daily Star*.

> Mrs Doreen Hill, the mother of the last of the thirteen murder victims, originally complained against the *Daily Star* but withdrew her complaint following a talk she and her solicitor had with Mr Lloyd Turner. Afterwards Mr Turner himself proposed that the Declaration should in future bar payments to the immediate relatives of persons engaged in crime. He later told the Council that despite the lack of support for his proposal when he had canvassed it with other editors, he put it forward for serious consideration.

Turner might have got away with this truly sickening humbug had not the *Sunday Times* and *Guardian* picked up on rumours emanating from the *Daily Star* that, in fact, Peter Sutcliffe's two brothers were being paid large sums by the paper at the same time as the editor was giving these sincere assurances to the Council and Mrs Doreen Hill. The total amount paid to the brothers was £26,500, far more than had been paid out by any other newspaper.

One wonders what went on in Turner's mind when faced with this humiliating exposure. His hypocrisy was there for all to see and yet, if the Press Council's account is anything to go by, he cared not one jot. Instead of just shutting up he began to justify these undisclosed contracts by saying that they enabled his newspaper to compile a dossier on the mistakes made by the police. He had the cheek to add that it was the publication of such dossiers which led to a Home Office inquiry. Clearly this did not impress the Council, which had no hesitation in condemning his evasion, his procrastination and his hypocrisy.

Thus in August 1983 the Council concluded its inquiries into the press conduct during the Ripper case. The different reports into newspaper activities do not on the whole provide a particularly edifying picture of the national press nor do they give one any great confidence in the judgment and ethical standards to be found in at least four national newspaper editors. The contradictions and omissions that they all made betrayed, I think, a calculated determination that the Press Council should not discover the truth, rather than carelessness or forgetfulness. While the Council was rightly congratulated on its long and arduous effort, the publicity that all this received did it no good at all. For it became quite clear to those who wish to place restraints on the press that had it not been for the fortuitous release of Mrs Sutcliffe's file of newspaper offers, little or none of the scandal would have emerged, and, more important, that the original complainant, Mrs Doreen Hill, would have gone away unsatisfied.

There is a considerable irony in this: on the one occasion that the Council fulfilled its constitutional aim of successfully dealing with a complaint, it provided arguments for those who want to bring in legislative controls. This, of course, does not help the Council fulfil its other constitutional aim: that of preserving the freedom of the press.

It is clear that the Council will never have any power. It is funded by newspaper proprietors, who are unlikely to endorse a system of fines that would penalise their own newspapers. Other suggestions, from abroad, include the suspension of offending journalists, but the Press Council views this as an infringement on an individual's right to earn a living and express himself. While there is not even any professional stigma attached to appearing in front of the Council, there seems little point in its existence.

CHAPTER 10

'Great is Truth and Mighty

Above all Things'

The *Sun*

Shortly before the Chesterfield by-election the *Sun* commissioned a psychiatrist to analyse the personality of the Labour candidate, Mr Tony Benn. The object, of course, was to confirm the newspaper's view that Mr Benn was mad, or at least to dissuade the Chesterfield electorate from voting for him. The newspaper's journalists assembled a 'dossier' of Mr Benn's main characteristics as they saw them and sent it to a Doctor David Hubbard, an American psychiatrist who later said that he was unaware that he was being asked to comment on a well-known British politician and that he did not know his remarks were being used in a newspaper. The 'analysis' duly appeared under the byline Martin Dunn and the headline, BENN ON THE COUCH:

> Some say Tony Benn is raving bonkers. But what really goes on in the complex mind of the country's most notorious left-winger?'

The newspaper promptly answered its own question by saying that he was far more than 'raving bonkers':

> He is a Messiah figure hiding behind the mask of the common man. He is greedy for power and will do anything to satisfy his hunger ... Tony Benn is a man driven by his own self-interest and thinks of himself as God.

Normally the paper would have got away with such a calculated slur, but fortuitously the *World in Action* programme had been monitoring the press coverage of the by-election and exposed the dishonest circumstances in which Mr Dunn's article had been written: namely, that Dr Hubbard said that he had spent little time on the consideration of Mr

Benn's personality and anyway it was quite obvious that the material assembled by the *Sun* was unlikely to be objective and even less likely to be of value in concluding his state of mind. Some days later the paper produced a defence in which it adopted the pose of the injured champion of truth, accused the programme of lying and even quoted the Bible in its favour: 'Great is truth and mighty above all things.'

It is possible to imitate the *Sun* by compiling a 'dossier' of the characteristics that Fleet Street exhibited in 1983 and make some conclusions as to its collective state of mind. There were, after all, many examples of erratic and unbalanced behaviour which, if displayed in an individual, would give a psychiatrist real cause for concern, demonstrating hallucinations produced by a mild paranoia, a derangement which causes the afflicted to believe in threats that do not exist and construct fantasies which confirm his beliefs. Of course, there were similar symptoms displayed in other newspapers. The *Sun* became convinced that an inoffensive social worker named Peter Tatchell was the greatest threat to Christendom since the Moorish invasion of Europe. Like the *News of the World*, the *Sunday Express*, the *Mail On Sunday* and to a lesser extent the *Daily Mail*, the *Sun* also took fright at the Peace Movement and was often unable to distinguish between fact and the manifestations of fear.

But it was in the *Daily Express* that this mental state was most pronounced for, even after the Press Council, the Ministry of Defence and the local authorities of Newbury took the trouble to correct its misapprehensions, the paper persisted in declaring that it was right while the rest of the world was wrong, grounds enough to incarcerate an individual in a quiet country home with a large supply of tranquillisers.

A variety of other conditions may be identified. The *Daily Star*, the *Sunday Mirror*, *Sunday People*, *Daily Mirror* and *News of the World* all continued to show signs of an unhealthy fixation on sexual matters. The *Sun* was especially susceptible and on one occasion even managed to find a sexual angle to politics:

'Women who vote SDP and Liberal are red-hot in bed . . . They not only have sex more often but they enjoy it more than their men.'

The tabloid press, like Walter Mitty, also exhibited compulsive dishonesty, inventing stories with no other object than to make itself appear interesting. Thus the *Daily Express* revealed the Duchess of Kent was to undergo electro-convulsive therapy, the *Sun* floated the possibility that Lord Olivier would take a part in *Coronation Street*, and the *News of the World* gave credence to all those absurd reports about UFOs landing in Suffolk and on the A5 in the Midlands.

It was clear on some occasions that reporters had simply become so confused that all hope of distinguishing fact from fiction had evaporated. How else could the *Daily Mirror* have announced on its front page that the Princess of Wales made regular visits to a little old lady when in fact she was attending a dancing class? How else could the *Sun* reporter have muddled an actor with his television personality throughout the report? There was also the odd outbreak of amnesia, especially at the *Sun*. On July 7, 1983, the newspaper rightly brought our attention to the fact that its rival, the *Daily Star*, had made up an interview with Mick Jagger. The paper quoted Mr Jagger as saying, 'I never even talked to the guy. Every word was made up.' Then it advised its readers, 'Best stick with the real thing, folks.' While the paper should be congratulated for this commendable concern for the truth, it is as well to remember that just eight months before it had carried an entirely bogus interview with Mrs Marica McKay.

So the diagnosis does not seem to offer much hope for the patient, especially when you consider that so much of the fraudulent activity of the popular press is commissioned with the conscious aim of damaging groups and individuals who do not conform to Fleet Street's own view of the way things should be.

A pro-Conservative bias is nothing new; however many Labour politicians and union leaders were utterly unprepared for the malevolence that greeted their efforts in the by-elections and general election of 1983. Whatever one's views, the wholehearted support for the political establishment in the last five years must be unhealthy. It is no coincidence that the worst journalistic misdemeanours occur in those papers which have given their unequivocal blessing to this government, that is to say the *Sun*, the *News of the World*, the *Daily Mail*, the *Mail on Sunday*, the *Daily Express* and the *Sunday Express*. True, there are lapses in papers of the Mirror group which broadly support the Labour party, but they are nowhere near as frequent or serious. The decline in standards is the product less of right-wing views than of intolerance. Once concessions are made in the reporting of politics and associated issues (concessions which are just as likely to be made by the dogmatic left) there is evidence that principles in other, unrelated areas of journalism are compromised.

Apart from conveying an accurate record of recent events to its readers, the first duty of the press is to represent the people, to put questions to the legislative and executive, to test the effectiveness of local and national government and to see that other influential forces in our society – labour and industrial combines, for instance – do not abuse their power to the detriment of the common good. This is made all the more difficult by the fact that governments, Whitehall, town halls, unions and big industry generally tend to the view that the public's interest is best served by ignorance while their own are best served by secrecy. A spirit of inquiry is therefore called for, a determination to lift what Peter Kellner of the *New Statesman* calls the 'tawdry mask' of the establishment. There are many journalists who with considerable skill effectively probe the establishment, Peter Hennessy of the *Times*, John Carvel of the *Guardian* and Paul Foot of the *Mirror*, to name a few, but generally Fleet Street, which likes to refer to itself as the Fourth Estate, has abdicated from this most important responsibility. Occasionally newspapers announce with a great deal of fuss that they are setting up investigative units, but these are usually in response to journalistic fashion rather than any real desire to serve the readership by making it better informed. In the late sixties and early seventies the *Sunday Times* operated perhaps the most successful such team that Fleet Street has ever seen. Although Insight was much ridiculed for its self-importance and boastful presentation it did properly represent the interests of the public and contributed much to the general debate on such issues as pollution, the responsibility of drug companies, cabinet secrecy, airline safety measures and the misbehaviour of property developers. The point about the publication of the results of such inquiries is that they not only increased knowledge but also produced changes in laws or regulations. Today, sadly, investigative journalism is either concerned with the trivial (the long-running inquiry by the *Sunday Times* into the importation of kangaroo meat and revelations about obscure and unimportant spies) or an instrument of a newspaper's political phobias (the 'inquiries' by the *Daily Mail*, *Daily Express* and the *Sun* into C.N.D. and Militant Tendency). During 1983 there were any number of stories which suggested that further investigation might be beneficial to the public interest. There were, for instance, persistent rumours that the nuclear processing plant at Sellafield (formerly Windscale) was leaking quantities of dangerous waste into the Irish Sea, and yet no newspaper mounted any serious effort to penetrate official secrecy and discover their substance. The year was characterised by the withdrawal of a number of arthritis and painkilling drugs which had been freely prescribed for many years and yet were suddenly discovered to be harmful and, in some cases, fatal. No newspaper to my certain knowledge resolved to discover the research that preceded mass manufacture of drugs like Opren and Distalgesic or to review the government safety measures. In financial journalism, the flotation of Reuters leaps to mind as a suitable case for investigation. There was however an extreme reluctance in all financial and City pages to mention the proposed sale and the abandonment of the Reuters Trust. This is probably explained by the fact that the newspaper proprietors stood to gain most from the secrecy of the operation. It was nonetheless in the general interest to reveal that such an important part of the communications business was to be flogged off without guarantees of its future integrity. After a year of silence it fell to Alexander Chancellor and Geoffrey Robertson to write the story in the *Spectator*, not normally known for its dedication to crusading journalism.

Often the instincts at the quality end of the market are right, only for a successful conclusion to an enquiry to be prevented by a failure of nerve, a lack of conviction or an awe of the establishment. This attitude was most clearly seen in the *Guardian*, which published the government's plans for the handling of Parliament and the press on the arrival of cruise missiles in Britain. Although these revelations could in no way be described as a threat to national security the newspaper allowed itself to be intimidated by the establishment into handing back the leaked document, with the result that it lost a good many people's confidence in its ability to protect its sources and to inquire on the public's behalf.

In the popular press this spirit of inquiry, which naturally requires elements of courage and patience, has long since been replaced by a harassment of defenceless individuals and an unseemly intrusion into their private lives. There is often in their attitude the identifiable psychology of the thug. For while the *Sun* and the *Daily Express* are perfectly content to bully the private citizens who come to their attention, neither would dream of taking on a powerful corporation or the government. 'Investigations' in the popular press call for little courage *or* patience. The most frequent example is the exposure of massage parlours which has become the speciality of the *News of the World* and the *Sunday People*. Clearly the people running these ill-disguised brothels are breaking the law, but this is never the reason for the monotonous stream of I-made-my-excuses-and-left stories. Rather it is a pretext for giving the reader a vicarious little thrill. Massage parlours are obviously not a threat to the public well-being or, for that matter, to a newspaper, which is what makes them such an easy target. Another soft option was Nikki Freud, the daughter of the Liberal M.P. for Ely, who, the *News of the World* learnt, dealt in cocaine. Alex Marunchak, the paper's reporter, encouraged one of her friends to introduce him as a potential buyer. This was how he announced the news:

> Nikki Freud, daughter of Liberal M.P. Clement Freud, is a top people's drug dealer. The attractive mother of two delivers cocaine – known as the champagne of drugs – to well-heeled clients all over London. In two deals the 31-year-old Miss Freud sold us cocaine – a total six grammes for £270.00.

While one does not condone drug dealing, it is as well to point out that this simple entrapment was only arranged in order to spread a well-known name over the pages of the *News of the World*. There was no concern for the evils of drug pushing; simply a desire for a sensational story. The judge presiding over Miss Freud's subsequent trial recognised this and criticised Marunchak and his accomplices, while the Attorney-General made it clear that in future journalists who incite such crimes would be liable to prosecution.

More often than not the popular press does away with reporting skills altogether by simply producing a cheque book. This expedient is increasingly used to tie up the participants of sensational stories in Exclusive contracts, thus inhibiting the free flow of information. The immediate reaction of most popular newspapers following the arrest of the Yorkshire Ripper was to try to buy up his relations. Nearly all, as we have seen, subsequently tried to conceal the extent of their dealings with these venal characters, especially when it was pointed out that they were breaking the Press Council's Declaration of Principle against the payment of potential witnesses. The Council's excellent report on their behaviour should have deterred newspapers, but it did not. The *Daily Mail* signed a contract with Miss Sue Stephens, a witness to the shooting of Stephen Waldorf, and the *Mail on Sunday*, while not infringing the Principle, showed extreme bad taste by buying the memoirs of Ronald Gregory, the former Chief Constable of Yorkshire. Mr Gregory was barely out of uniform before his unenlightening thoughts on the Ripper hunt were gracing the pages of the paper. What made this expensive serialisation particularly unpleasant were two things: first, Mr Gregory had barred his officers from giving lengthy interviews to the press and himself had declined to talk to a journalist from the *Sheffield Morning Telegraph* who had approached him without an offer of money. Second, Mr Stewart Steven, Sir David English's prodigy and editor of the *Mail on Sunday*, defended criticism by claiming that it was in the public interest that Mr Gregory's valuable testament should be published. This might have convinced people if Mr Gregory had given freely of his experience and if his 'memoirs' had not been so lurid and repetitive. The Press Council saw the light: 'The publication so soon after the dreadful series of murders and attacks must have been acutely distressing to the relatives of those killed and to the victims who survived.'

The Press Council does not agree that the publication disclosed anything of sufficient public interest to outweigh the mischief of its publication.

Even if we were to ignore Fleet Street's inability to inquire, there is little satisfaction to be obtained in the performance of its other main role, the publication of an accurate record of events. Of course there were many cases of excellent reporting during 1983, particularly in the quality papers' coverage of the Middle East and Central America, but generally the standards were abysmally low. Accuracy, as we have seen, was frequently lost in the desire to entertain, to promote some message or to indulge in fantasy. Often the most basic information, such as ages and the spelling of names, is wrong. Quotations cannot be relied upon either, for they are often exaggerated to achieve some effect or simply approximated because the journalist cannot be bothered to get them right.

Another way in which the newspapers persistently intervene between the reader and the truth is their use of language. On the last day of 1983 the *Times* addressed itself to George Orwell's *1984* and correctly observed that the author was more concerned with the use of words than with political systems. The frightening idea at the centre of the book is that the range of thought may be narrowed by the gradual elimination of vocabulary so that eventually ideas disappear because the words to express them no longer exist. The *Times* leader noted that both by design and default there was a progressive and irrecoverable deterioration in the use of language:

Language is to public discourse and private morality what a sound currency is to economic stability: once it is subverted, society will lose its touchstone, and even its symbols and myths which are normally conveyed through the words and are part of every society's self-consciousness.

It is a characteristic of every age to decry a decline in standards. But the decline in the respect for language, and its subversion by some and traducement by many others, has a particular warning for us, because it will diminish and ultimately destroy our ability to perceive ... and we will no longer be capable of just expression and fair evaluation.

Nowhere in this long and otherwise commendable article did the author consider the dangers of the daily 'subversion' and 'traducement' of the language in the press. It would be going too far to say that *Sun* or *Daily Star* readers have been robbed of their ability to think, but certainly someone who relies on these newspapers for the majority of his information will have a very narrow understanding of events and issues. This is partly because the notions expressed never attempt to be more than crude approximations, but more so because popular newspapers are incapable of conveying news in moderate language. Stories are pumped up with hyperbolic words like 'mob', 'riot', 'shock', 'chaos', 'trauma', 'miracle', 'wonder' and 'tragedy' when their moderate counterparts 'crowd', 'protest', 'surprise', 'disorder', 'ordeal', 'luck' and 'sadness' will tell you much more accurately what has happened. Newspapers also use language as an effective weapon against those they wish to discredit. Thus 'chaos' is used to describe a few arrests at demonstrations, unemployment protestors march 'on' rather than 'to' London, and the *Daily Mail* reported that the Conservatives 'won' seats in the last election while Labour 'grabbed' them, the implication being that the Conservatives had a rightful claim in every constituency in the country while Labour must have been extremely underhand to gain any at all.

Fleet Street arrived at the end of 1983 never having served its public quite so badly. Newspapers had lied to entertain, to compete with each other, to propagate their political convictions and to persecute those with whom they disagreed. And when there was no other obvious reason journalists continued to lie simply out of habit. The editors were no better. Two allowed themselves to be bamboozled into endorsing the obvious work of sinister confidence tricksters, four did everything in their power to deceive the body that is charged with protecting the freedom of the press, another had crumpled in the face of official pressure and released material which incriminated his paper's source, and others involved their papers in financial deals of such grandiose stupidity that their fitness to run national newspapers must surely be called into question. With the exception of the *Guardian* and the *Sunday Times*, which at least made some public atonement for their incompetence, there was little remorse displayed either. Newspapers are organisations which are concerned with the moment, and thus the preoccupations of the people who work in them are necessarily immediate. As a rule, editors and their journalists are not given to introspection nor afflicted by any great doubts in life. And so they proceeded into 1984 with their minds fixed on bingo promotion and the circulation war and their memories rapidly eliminating all the unfortunate episodes of 1983.

But there is cause enough for concern. For while the quality newspapers are more tentative and less adventurous than I can ever remember them, something decidedly unpleasant is beginning to emerge in the popular press (except, perhaps, in the *Daily Mirror*). It is difficult to pin down, but I think it is best expressed by a meanness of spirit, a lack of aspiration and a contempt for the suffering that their own activities undoubtedly cause. Journalists usually reply by quoting either H.L. Mencken to the effect that nobody lost money underestimating the intelligence of the public, or that old cliché about the public getting the press it deserves. They argue that the bad taste and dishonesty are all desired by readers, who would otherwise stop buying newspapers. Since newspapers do not publicise their deceptions their readers are hardly in a position to decide whether or not to take their custom elsewhere. It seems perfectly possible for a newspaper to be popular as well as honest, inquiring and informative. Thus the public does not get the press it deserves.

So what hope is there for an improvement in standards? Some may be bound in the Mirror Group's plan to launch a new popular daily which would promote the Labour and union viewpoint. The left is under-represented in Fleet Street and the balance undoubtedly needs to be redressed, but it is said that the paper has not been conceived out of a desire for dispassionate reporting. Fresh competition to the established Fleet Street newspapers is most certainly needed. Advances in printing technology, which could radically cut the costs of publishing a newspaper, may help. However, the introduction of new newspapers by outsiders would require the blessing of a number of powerful Fleet Street unions, and for the moment it suits them and the proprietors to maximise newspapers' income by limiting competition.

Ultimately, then, we must hope for some benign intervention from the proprietors, who are still the strongest influence on the national press. Cynics will suggest that this is a vain hope; in the past they have displayed a greater concern for the commercial viability of their products than for their integrity. However, they may be able to recognise something which their editors have conspicuously failed to do; that unless newspapers improve their standards they will at some time indubitably become the subject of legislation which will permanently injure the freedom of the press.

The Men
Who Run Fleet Street

ASSOCIATED NEWSPAPERS
Daily Mail; Mail on Sunday

LORD ROTHERMERE: PROPRIETOR

The tycoon proprietors lay a great deal less stress on the need for continuity in their newspapers than the old press-owning families. Like Lord Hartwell at the *Daily Telegraph*, Lord Rothermere, the proprietor of Associated Newspapers, favours a consistency of view and relative permanence in the key appointments of his organisation. He often boasts that the political views of the *Daily Mail*, which was founded by the brilliant creator of popular journalism, Lord Northcliffe, have not changed for nearly eighty years. There is some truth in this, even if during the 1930s the paper exhibited distinctly fascist tendencies. Today the *Daily Mail* under Rothermere, the great grand-nephew of the first Lord Northcliffe, is less extreme, but is no less fervent in its support of free enterprise and conservatism and its opposition to union and parts of the welfare state.

Rothermere has intelligently run his inheritance with tried and trusted subordinates, notably Sir David English, the Editor of the *Daily Mail*, and Mick Shields, the financial brain behind the success of some of the group's other interests. Even when David English offered his resignation during the Leyland letter débâcle (see English, below), Lord Rothermere sensibly resisted pressure to accept it in the knowledge that English was one of the best editors of his generation.

Despite such wise delegation, Lord Rothermere gets a very bad press indeed. It is often assumed, for instance, that his somewhat irrational and impulsive manner comes from his uncle, the last Lord Northcliffe, who died raving mad, claiming to his employees that he had been poisoned by German ice cream. His life-style is generally held to be that of a rich absentee landlord, who has little interest in his newspapers other than their profitability.

Rothermere was born in 1925 and christened Vere Harmsworth. He was educated at Eton, but failed to pass into Sandhurst. He was dispatched by his father to Canada to work as a lumberjack with Anglo-Canadian paper mills. In 1957 he married a vivacious chorus girl named Beverley Brooks, known to her friends as Bubbles. Her main contribution to the newspaper industry has been to supply unlimited material for gossip columnists. Rothermere's knowledge of the newspaper industry, though nothing like as extensive as Lord Hartwell's, was acquired by working his way up Associated Newspapers to become Vice Chairman under his father. When, in 1971, he was given complete control of the group, he displayed an unexpected boldness. He sanctioned the merger of the *Daily Sketch* with the *Daily Mail* and launched the *Mail* as a tabloid, a move that the *Daily Express* was forced to follow. He revamped the *Evening News*, and when that failed to stop losses he buried his pride and arranged a merger with the *Evening Standard*, which was owned by Express Newspapers. Once rid of the *News*, Rothermere turned his attention to the Sunday market and launched the *Mail on Sunday* with the intention of taking readers from both the *Sunday Express* and the *Sunday Times*. (He described the *Mail on Sunday* as being between the haughties and naughties.)

Against David English's advice he entrusted the launch of the paper to Bernard Shrimsley, a former editor of the *News of the World*. It was not a success and for a moment the paper looked as if it was going to replace the *Evening News* as the big loss-making asset on Associated's books. Rothermere was quickly persuaded to fire Shrimsley and instal English with a crisis squad from the *Mail*. While the paper was undoubtedly saved, it still loses money under Stewart Steven.

Rothermere's main fault is that he reacts to his paper as a reader and not a proprietor. He recognises a good product well enough but has none of the journalistic instincts which a good proprietor should, in part, possess. This is not to say that he does not interfere with the running of the paper. On the advice of Sir James Goldsmith he wrote to the Diarist, Nigel Dempster, saying that Dempster's column was like 'a dish of cold potatoes' and threatening to fire him. Dempster was saved by English, who spoke up on his behalf, but on other occasions Rothermere has had his way. It must not be forgotten that the *Daily Mail* is one of the most biased newspapers in Fleet Street, especially at election time when it becomes propagandist in its support of the Conservative Party. Rothermere is not a man of sophisticated political views. His support for the Conservative Party is inbred; he would no more consider transferring his papers' allegiance to the Labour Party than he would consider taking Bubbles to Butlin's.

SIR DAVID ENGLISH: EDITOR, *Daily Mail*

Sir David English wrote in 1977, 'The *Daily Mail* published on its front page an extract from a letter which it believed at the time to have been written by Lord Ryder. But this later proved to be false.' There then followed a positively heart-rending 500-word public atonement – up to a point. At the end of English's fluent apology there is an interesting attempt to divert his readers' attention from the negligence of the *Daily Mail* with the following thought: 'There is genuine and deserved criticism and anger. But on top of that there is the ugly bullyboy campaign of intimidation and fear . . . we can take the first. The second is an orchestrated campaign to silence us.' Who were these nameless bullies? English does not identify them, but the reader is left with the impression that very sinister influences were at work and that the freedom of the press itself was threatened.

There was, of course, no campaign of intimidation or fear; rather, some strong and pertinent attacks on a paper which had distinguished itself in the hostile pursuit of the Labour Party and was so rooted in its bias that English and his deputies gave no more than a cursory glance to what was an obvious fake. The article was a typical example of English turning the situation to his favour. The *Daily Mail* readers, never noted for their great insight, obeyed the implicit request for support and wrote in their hundreds to the paper.

David English is a very talented journalist indeed, and this episode served to show his colleagues in Fleet Street that he possessed a capacity to survive too. He was born into a respectable middle-class family in Bournemouth in 1931. He was a bright and thrusting child and did well at the local school. Although there was no history of journalism in his family (his father was an accountant), he promptly applied to the *Bournemouth Echo* on leaving school. By the age of twenty-one he was a reporter in Fleet Street with the *Daily Mirror*. He worked for short spells on the *Daily Mail*, *Daily Sketch*, the *Dispatch* and finally landed a job as American correspondent for the *Daily Express*. He covered the 1960 and 1964 presidential campaigns admirably and came to know President Kennedy. In 1965 English was given control of the *Express* Foreign Desk, then a much more important job than it is today, and proved himself to be good at organisation and applying pressure where it counts. English returned to America to organise the coverage of the 1968 Presidential election and produced an instant account of Richard Nixon's victory called *Divided They Stand*. He was passed over for promotion at the *Daily Express* and in the same year went to the *Daily Sketch* as Editor. It's a testament to English's skill as an office politician that when the *Sketch* was merged with the *Daily Mail* in the latter's favour, he and the staff he had come to know at the *Sketch* ended up on top of the pile in the revamped *Daily Mail*. Unlike many journalists, English has an eye for a good commercial proposition. He imported the launderette idea from America in the sixties and set up a little stable of freesheet newspapers. Both businesses were sold at a profit.

David English's achievement at the *Daily Mail* is incontestable, whatever one's politics. He took a rapidly decaying institution and with an astute perception of his market created a formula which has attracted some 1.8 million readers every day for the last decade. In view of the professionalism of the *Mail*, it is rather surprising that the paper has not gained more readers from the *Daily Express*, which in the same period has procrastinated about its style and market. The atmosphere within the *Daily Mail* is highly competitive. It is frequently the case that two or even three writers are commissioned to fill a particular feature page in the following day's paper. The writers, not always aware of each other's efforts, duly turn in their pieces and the best is chosen. Among Fleet Street reporters, the *Mail*'s News Desk has the reputation of being the most despotic and bloody-minded. Journalists are pushed to produce a story where there is often none. The result, it goes without saying, is that the accuracy of the paper is not all that one would wish for, and the scruples of the journalists are few.

English thrives on the competitiveness of his underlings and actively encourages his staff in their manoeuvrings, a pleasure which he may have first learned at Beaverbrook's *Daily Express*. He is the willing recipient of office and Street gossip and is known for the charm and gusto with which he induces indiscretion. In Fleet Street he has a small group of friends who are mostly on his paper. Outside journalism, he is said to have an unblemished private life. He has been married since 1954, has three children and enjoys skiing and sailing. The most interesting thing his journalists have dug up about him is that he once had a passion for ballroom dancing.

It is, perhaps, the background of somebody who does not suffer great intellectual or moral doubts and who is capable of considerable self-righteousness. I quote from that same article in 1977: 'Does anyone believe that if we had had a Tory Government for the past three years, this paper would have been a sycophantic lapdog silently adoring our rulers with moist and worshipping eyes?'

The answer to the question, I think, lies in the knighthood Mr English accepted from Mrs Thatcher.

STEWART STEVEN: EDITOR, *Mail on Sunday*
When the *Daily Mail* came to announce the elevation of Mr Stewart Steven to the editorship of the *Mail on Sunday*, it was remarkably coy about his career. We learnt that he was forty-five, had started as the Political Correspondent of the *Western Daily Press* and Central Features, had moved to the *Daily Express* as a Lobby Correspondent in 1964 and was promoted to Diplomatic Correspondent in 1965. He became Foreign Editor in 1967 and Assistant Editor of the *Daily Mail*

in 1973. This auspicious rise was matched by the publication of three books, the most recent of which is on Poland, and a happy marriage. Sir David English was quoted by the anonymous author of the story to say that Steven was 'a great journalist and would be an outstanding editor'.

Steven is a lot more interesting than this rather bland account makes him out to be. What it did not say was that on two occasions in his professional life Steven has had every reason to regret his chosen career. The first was at the *Daily Express* when, as Foreign Editor, Steven had investigated a claim that the Nazi war criminal Martin Bormann was alive and living in South America. After exhaustive enquiries he announced that Hitler's deputy had been found. That front page must rank among the most embarrassing that the *Daily Express* has ever printed, for within a matter of days rival newspapers proved that the only person Steven had found was a rather bewildered South American carpenter; furthermore, he had been taken for a ride by a notorious con-man.

The second occasion came in 1977, by which time Steven had moved to join his friend David English at the *Daily Mail* as Assistant Editor. In the spring of that year he was charged with the job of investigating claims that Lord Ryder had set up a slush fund at British Leyland. In their enthusiasm for the story, Steven and the other journalists working on the story ignored the many obvious flaws in the letters and documents that had been given to the paper as evidence. The hoax was again quickly exposed. This time however, the consequences were a great deal more serious. The entire parliamentary Labour Party condemned the *Daily Mail* while the Labour politicians Eric Varley and Lord Ryder filed writs for libel. Steven tendered his resignation. For a while it looked as if he might become the *Mail*'s scapegoat, but in the end his friend the editor stood by him.

During the painful days following the story Steven insisted that his judgment had in no way been affected by a wish to compromise the Labour Party; in fact, he said, he was a lifelong supporter. There is certainly very little evidence of this in his time at the *Mail* and even less during his editorship of the *Mail on Sunday*.

Steven was never the first choice for Lord Rothermere's new Sunday paper. Against the advice of Sir David English and his executives, he installed the former editor of the *News of the World*, Bernard Shrimsley, and a team of journalists who were nowhere near as skilled as their counterparts at the *Daily Mail*. Predictably and, one suspects, for Sir David gratifyingly, the experiment was a disaster. Nine weeks after the launch Shrimsley resigned and Sir David moved in with a squad of executives

Undoubtedly the greatest influence in Steven's professional life has been his friendship with Sir David. Without this it seems unlikely that he would have been made editor of a national newspaper. In his attitude and tastes Steven is still very much a product of the *Daily Mail* school; two years after his appointment the *Mail on Sunday* bears the unmistakable stamp of Sir David. Steven, though, is beginning to strike out on his own and is prepared to fight his own battles.

EXPRESS NEWSPAPERS
Daily Express; Sunday Express; Daily Star

LORD MATTHEWS: CHAIRMAN AND CHIEF EXECUTIVE

There is little in Lord Matthews's background to suggest that he was either suitable or ambitious for the position of Chairman and Chief Executive of the Express Newspapers group. He was born in Islington, North London, in 1919; his father was killed in the last months of the First World War. Although his education was limited to an elementary school near Highbury, he seems to have been imbued by his mother with a strong work ethic and determination to succeed. His ambition took some while to exhibit itself. He worked as an office boy in a tobacco company and in 1939 joined the Navy as an ordinary seaman. After the war he spent ten years steadily working up the management of the building firm Trollope and Colls. Not until 1960, by which time Matthews and his wife Joyce had settled comfortably into the middle class, did he decide to risk his career and capital of £2500 by purchasing a small building concern in South London. By 1964, the time of his fortunate meeting with Nigel Broackes, he had quadrupled the turnover of his firm to £1 million a year.

Broackes, a debonair thirty-year-old who had been educated at Stowe and commissioned into the Third Hussars, was impressed by Matthews's ability as a manager and entrepreneur. Three years later they sealed their unlikely friendship in a merger of their separate companies, and Matthews became managing director of Trafalgar House. The story since then has been one of spectacular success. In 1979 Nigel Broackes wrote in his autobiography *A Growing Concern* that he and Matthews had built a conglomerate worth a conservative billion pounds in little under twelve years.

When Sir Max Aitken decided to sell off his inheritance in 1977 there were many more obvious purchasers than Broackes and Matthews. Rupert Murdoch had expressed a definite interest and had even gone so far as to write out a cheque to Sir Max for £1.4 million, Vere Harmsworth of Associated Newspapers was naturally keen to buy up the *Mail*'s old competitor, and both Sir James Goldsmith and Tiny Rowland had indicated their willingness to be considered. After long and some would say typically agonised procrastination Aitken eventually decided to sell to Trafalgar, by far the richest, but by no means the most experienced of the suitors.

Matthews has since revealed that it took Nigel Broackes a full month to persuade him that Trafalgar could sort out the dire problems of the group, which then consisted of the *Daily Express*, the *Sunday Express* and the *Evening Standard*. 'I knew I would be the one who had to run them and that was why I was reluctant,' Matthews has said. Broackes presents it another way; he wrote in *A Growing Concern* that he wanted to get the 'morose and morbid' Victor out of the office and 'once again engrossed in a new challenge'. At the time this caused one of the very few public disagreements in their association, but eventually both agreed that they had bought the paper for patriotic reasons; a strong theme in Trafalgar House's expansion has been the purchase of names such as Cunard and The Ritz, strongly redolent of Britain's imperial past. 'I believe very much that standards should be as I recall them in the pre-war days when Britain was a top nation and respected, and you were proud of it. And I hate to see these things disappear, or anything that reflects that era,' Matthews said to *Campaign* magazine. (Incidentally, this worthy sentiment clearly does not extend to architecture of the period; the Firestone building on the outskirts of London was pulled down by Matthews's company before the authorities had time to put a preservation order on it.)

It is fair to say that when Matthews moved into the shiny black building which his old firm Trollope and Colls had built for Beaverbrook, he had only the crudest notions of what journalism and the newspaper industry were about. He decided, sensibly in view of this ignorance, to treat the Express Group as he would any other ailing company, seeing it purely in terms of balance sheets, labour relations, management and assets, which all looked decidedly unhealthy in 1977. While other proprietors spent their time talking about their newspaper's policy in public and retired to the privacy of their boardrooms to consider possible mergers and closures, Matthews openly discussed his newspapers as a product. If they did not sell or had no potential for profit, he would, quite simply cease to manufacture them. Here is part of a conversation between the BBC journalist Richard Kershaw and Matthews, broadcast in 1979:

Kershaw: Would you still close the *Express* or perhaps the *Standard* if it was necessary, because they were not profitable?

Matthews: Oh yes, quite definitely.

Kershaw: We are talking about newspapers as money, and almost like a commodity. How do you look at newspapers though, otherwise?

Matthews: May I say that's how I look at newspapers? As money.

He expressed much the same views about editors. 'Think of a football manager and put editors in the same category. I suspect football managers change more often than our editors. But if you get the package right, the editor is there for life.' In other words he is quick to dispose of an editor who he feels is not getting the package right, as Derek Jameson and his successor at the *Daily Express*, Christopher Ward, will readily confirm.

Nearly all Matthews's views and tastes are subjugated to his need to make money. When he launched the *Daily Star* in 1979, his aim was to reduce the Group's overheads rather than to make any significant contribution to the British media. He has often said himself that the *Star* would be the very last paper he'd buy in the morning. Matthews is a rather simple builder with modest enough tastes and plain, old-fashioned values. He has often been perplexed by the ways of Fleet Street and on several occasions has considered selling the *Express*. But he has gained a certain prestige, some wealth and, of course, a life peerage for his loyal support of the Conservative party in the 1979 election.

SIR LARRY LAMB: EDITOR, *Daily Express*

Sir Larry Lamb is a Yorkshireman. While I hesitate to ascribe to him all the characteristics of the stereotype, his background goes a fair way to explaining his personality. He was born in 1929 to a poorish mining family in the village of Fitzwilliam, where his father was the local colliery blacksmith. His education was superficial and he has always maintained that the generation educated in the war was deprived of good teachers. His hopes, ambitions and socialist affiliation were instilled in him by his family. On leaving school he wanted to become a journalist but failed, owing to the large numbers of men looking for work after the war. Instead he took a job as a cashier in Brighouse Town Hall and diverted his energy into the union, NALGO, eventually becoming a stroppy branch secretary. After a time on his union's paper, he moved rapidly through a string of sub-editing jobs, eventually landing a position on the *Evening Standard*. These, together with his subsequent moves to the *Daily Mail*, to the *Mirror* and back to the *Daily Mail*, displayed an intense desire to get on. During his first spell at the *Mail* he achieved a certain fame by impaling himself in the forehead with a spike, the sub-editors' upturned nail on which rejected stories are placed. Happily the spike was removed in hospital and Lamb suffered no lasting physical scars except, perhaps, a tendency thereafter to respect the low brow.

In 1969 Lamb was asked by Rupert Murdoch to become editor of the

Sun, which the Mirror group had just sold off for £60,000. The success of the Murdoch–Lamb combination is now legend in Fleet Street and proves that Murdoch has at least been able to work with an editor over a long period of time. The two apparently got on well; both are reserved, hard-working and determined. Together they developed a formula which was to dictate how the *Daily Mirror* and latterly the *Star* were to develop. Lamb introduced the Page Three pin-up, enlarged the headlines, condensed copy and concentrated on the sort of sensation which has now spread to other parts of Murdoch's empire. In a matter of months the paper began to eat away at the *Mirror*'s circulation. In 1977 it overtook its complacent and worthy rival and now, with a circulation of over 4 million, contributes some £15 million a year to News International.

One of the more baffling aspects of Sir Larry during the *Sun*'s rise was his view that he was in quality journalism. Not content with the most rapid expansion in the history of Fleet Street, he went about insisting that the *Sun* had as high a regard for truth and information as *The Times*. His own journalists, however, continued to call the paper the *Beano*. Lamb reacts badly to criticism and got into the habit of dispatching mean letters through his lawyers to people who attacked the *Sun*. Bill Grundy, then the *Spectator*'s regular press columnist, was the recipient on several occasions. 'I think he did it because he is a prickly Yorkshireman,' observed Grundy in 1976. 'His trouble is that he has an extraordinary loyalty to the paper. He sees it as a crusading journal, a bulwark of freedom even.'

This loyalty, although a strong element in Lamb's character, did not apply to socialism. Shortly before the 1979 election Larry Lamb became convinced of Mrs Thatcher's quality, and he urged his readers to vote Conservative. It is questionable how much influence such editorials have; however, Mrs Thatcher seems to have believed in it enough to reward Lamb with a knighthood.

Lamb eventually left in 1981 and disappeared to Australia to edit a couple of newspapers. Two years later he was bored and, like Derek Jameson and Christopher Ward before him, wrote to Lord Matthews asking for an editorship. As it happened Matthews was disillusioned with Ward's performance and had recently received a number of memoranda from senior staff on the *Express* confirming his opinion. Ward was unceremoniously recalled from holiday, given £80,000 and told that he was being replaced by Lamb. The effect was immediately noticeable. The paper plunged down-market with bold, sensational and often inaccurate stories all decorated with the boastful headlines that Lamb had pioneered at the *Sun*. The paper has, it is true, gained in circulation but this is the result of the *Express* Millionaires Club, an ingenious variation of newspaper bingo dreamt up by Lamb. The chances of winning are slim indeed, and it has been suggested that one is more likely to get a large sum of money from the *Daily Express* by becoming Editor and then being fired.

Recently he offered his resignation over the affair of the fake Scargill speech; when one considers the unlikelihood of the proprietor of a conservative newspaper – Lord Matthews – allowing a trade unionist the right of reply, this is perhaps not surprising. For the time being, he is still there.

SIR JOHN JUNOR: EDITOR, *Sunday Express*

Sir John Junor, the Editor of the *Sunday Express* for thirty years, once rang his Northern Editor and asked what he thought of his own current events column in the previous issue of the paper. 'It was wonderful,' replied the unfortunate executive, 'just as wonderful and to the point as ever.'

'Rubbish,' Junor said, 'it was piss-poor and you know it.' The exchange continued in this manner for a few minutes with both parties holding their ground. Eventually Junor hung up and the sweating employee returned to his colleagues, who all congratulated him on his brave defiance of Junor.

Such stories about Junor are legion and enjoyed as much by Fleet Street as by the subject himself. Junor has gone to great lengths to cultivate the image of an eccentric and unpredictable despot. There are very few areas in which Junor does not hold some unshakably bizarre opinion. He once asked a young reporter how much his shoes cost. The reporter, not wanting to offend the notorious parsimony of his editor, replied that he had bought them for a mere £4. With a look of the utmost severity Junor said, 'Let me give you a word of advice laddie. It is a false economy to buy cheap shoes.' These words of advice often conflict from day to day and it is generally suspected that he uses them to unsettle rather than benefit his staff. He is said, for instance, to have lectured the same reporter at a later stage on the extravagance and wastefulness of buying expensive shoes. In his time he has decreed that white wine and rosé are only drunk by poofs, a group of people whose moral turpitude Junor believes is solely responsible for the decline of our civilisation. He has also, as Alan Watkins recalls in his *Brief Lives*, delivered himself of the view that sex was quite out of the question in the morning. One wonders where he gets these strange views. In part he has obviously modelled himself on that old tyrant Lord Beaverbrook, who rejoiced in the perversity of his opinions, but there is also a strong presbyterian streak in Junor. He was born in 1919, the third son of a working-class family in Glasgow. His forbears had moved there from Black Isle, Ross and Cromarty. Like his current proprietor, Lord Matthews, he grew up in straitened circumstances which were not helped by the huge unemployment of the depression. Encouraged by their mother, the three sons did well at school and headed towards the professions, the traditional escape-route for the working classes. While Junor's brothers became a doctor and a headmaster, he displayed an early and fervent interest in the Liberal Party. He retained his parliamentary ambitions throughout his twenties and thirties and contested three by-elections, in Aberdeen (1945), Edinburgh (1948) and Dundee (1951) – all for the Liberals.

He was introduced to journalism quite by chance. When serving as Lieutenant in the Fleet Air Arm, he was instructed to start up a morale-boosting newspaper for his colleagues stationed in Lancashire. He was an inspired choice and by 1945 Junor was editing the Fleet Air Arm's national magazine. After a brief spell in the London bureau of the *Sydney Sun*, Junor was spotted by Beaverbrook and nine years later, at the age of thirty-five, was appointed editor of the *Sunday Express*. (It was one of Beaverbrook's qualities that young and talented journalists were given the opportunity to edit while they were still fresh.) Once installed at the *Sunday Express*, Junor proved hard to dislodge. Beaverbrook often hinted that the *Daily Express* was there for Junor's asking, but he always ignored the suggestions, preferring the familiarity and easy régime of the Sunday paper. Junor and Beaverbrook were close though they did fall out over Suez and the Profumo affair. On both occasions Junor criticised the Conservative governments.

Junor is as opinionated in his column (latterly Current Events) as he is in conversation. He is frequently in trouble with the libel and contempt of court laws, and he has appeared in front of the Press Council more than any other editor. The complaints that his remarks are in bad taste or display unusual bigotry, or even racism, are often upheld. He was the last editor to be summoned to the Bar of the House of Commons to answer allegations of contempt. It was a ludicrous performance in which Junor was made to apologise to the House for his observation during the Suez crisis that M.P.s' petrol tanks were brimming over while the rest of the country was suffering under petrol rationing. While Junor must be admired for his fearlessness it is doubtful whether he would let any member of his staff outrage quite so many parts of the establishment or, indeed, make so free with the paper's reputation and funds. Both Beaverbrook and Matthews have tolerated him because his paper has consistently contributed large profits to the group, although its circulation has declined radically from over five million in the early fifties to two and three quarter million in the 1980s.

With the exception of the eccentric fulminations of Junor's leader page, the *Sunday Express* is a remarkably bland product. The front page is usually led by some unexciting political story written for the most part in support of the Conservative Party. Inside readers are confronted with an unchanging formula of star interviews, war reminiscences and photographs of pretty girls whose main attribute is their decent attire. The news story, or rather stories that are presented as news, conform to an old convention whereby a good deal of unnecessary space is given over to long and picturesque descriptions.

Junor is now at the age when most editors are pensioned off, but there is no sign that Lord Matthews, who was also born in 1919, has any plans to entrust the profitable *Sunday Express* to younger, less certain hands. It is very likely that Junor will continue for at least another five years. His remarkable career was officially recognised by Mrs Thatcher with a knighthood in the New Year's Honours List of 1980. He has indeed survived longer than any other editor in living memory and he can honestly claim to have spoken his mind for the last thirty years. But has this mind been worth listening to? Are not the views and morals that Junor has purveyed every Sunday for the last three decades merely the echoes of the prejudices and instincts of an aging readership? Is there not in his homespun philosophy and sentimentality something really rather crass, stupid even? As Junor says, 'It is not libellous to ask a question.'

LLOYD TURNER: EDITOR, *Daily Star*

It must be rather disheartening to be editor of a national newspaper which has been created solely to cut the costs of a large group of newspapers. More so when you consider that the proprietor of Express Newspapers persistently voices his distaste for the unlovely child of his ownership. On any criterion you care to take Mr Lloyd Turner, the editor of the *Star* since 1980, has been less than successful. The circulation, for instance, has after soaring briefly returned to the figure that he inherited from his enthusiastic predecessor Derek Jameson. This was partly due to the political *volte-face* the paper performed before the last General Election. During the first Thatcher government Turner had spent much time insisting that the paper was devoted to improving the lot of the horny-handed sons of toil. The policy went down well with the staff, who were genuinely enthusiastic about dissent from the traditional policies of the group, and with the readership in the North of England, the paper's chief market. However, come the 1983 General Election, Turner, acting on the instructions of Lord Matthews, suddenly backed the Conservative party in a Polling Day article. It is of course perfectly within the right of Lloyd Turner and Lord Matthews to recommend whichever party they like; however it was a trifle dishonest to build up the circulation by appealing to traditional Labour supporters only to change loyalties at the last moment. Turner was, in fact, against the change of line and it was a pity that he did not put up more of a case for his argument to Lord Matthews.

The chief criticism, though, of Turner's editorship must be the lack of novelty in his paper. Rather than providing a contrast to its main rivals the *Daily Mirror* and the *Sun*, the *Daily Star* imitates them. Essentially its formula derives from the successful prototype created at the *Sun* by Larry Lamb in the late sixties. But as with all imitations it lacks conviction and authority. After four years Lloyd Turner should have done something to change this.

Turner was born in Australia in 1938. He came to Britain in his twenties to seek work as a journalist. After a period of successful freelance work he joined the *Daily Express* in 1968. During the troubled decade that followed, in which the *Daily Express* was subjected to a succession of editors, was converted into a tabloid and was sold to Trafalgar House, Turner steadily rose to become Night Editor, a moderately influential position which calls for a good grasp of newspaper production. At the time he was known for his colourful behaviour and a journalistic competence. Unusually for a rising executive, he became involved in the National Union of Journalists and held several positions at chapel (branch) level. These duties do not always seem to have been carried out with the greatest efficiency.

It is fair to say that Lloyd Turner is not popular among his staff at the *Daily Star*. Although the majority of them do not have daily contact with him because the paper's main office is in Manchester, many believe that he simply does not possess the qualities of an editor.

They say that he is too inconsistent in his views, and that he is bereft of workable ideas. His survival as editor is put down to his ability to disassociate himself from disasters. However, after the huge losses made on the Diana Dors diet and the humiliating exposure over the Ripper payments, the Express management may be beginning to look for a new editor.

THE GUARDIAN TRUST

PETER PRESTON: EDITOR, *Guardian*

Enigmatic is the word that always occurs in a description of Peter Preston, the 46-year-old editor of the *Guardian*, though this is probably due more to his shyness than any discernible mystery in his personality. Friends who have known him since he started work on what was the *Manchester Guardian* in 1963 are constantly astonished at his unwillingness to commit himself in conversation further than a shrug or a grunt. Nearly all recall occasions when Preston, having asked them to lunch at one of the two modest Greek tavernas he frequents, has sat in complete and unembarrassed silence for the entire meal. His path to the top of the *Guardian* was relatively smooth and reflects his qualities as an all-rounder. He progressed with ease from political correspondent to education correspondent, diary editor, features editor and finally to production editor. Many have observed that his diffidence, together with a certain executive caution, increased as he rose. Though it may not be consciously designed to do so, his reserve has the effect of keeping his staff at a safe distance – which is always useful for an editor.

Under his control, which began in 1975 after a rather curious process of consultation, the paper has steadily improved its circulation, finding for itself a readership which trusted its coverage and liked the emphasis on liberal and social causes. It is evidence of this success that the word *Guardian* is frequently used as an adjective. Interestingly the paper's strong identity is due, not to a firm imposition of Preston's values, but rather to his gift for spotting good journalists and letting them develop in relative freedom.

People frequently attest to his patience in waiting for a new feature or regular column to mature. He is one of Fleet Street's best delegators; he does not feel the need to pretend to the omniscience that others acquire with an editor's chair. He is, however, quick to absorb the facts and arguments of any given story, and is always familiar with the contents of his paper.

Preston's reserve may in part be due to the disabilities he suffered as a result of catching polio when a child. Were it not for these, which are more considerable than they appear, he would probably have been a keen and talented sportsman. As it is, he is a passionate football supporter and will spend many winter Saturdays on the terraces watching Charlton or Millwall. His other chief interest is the film business, about which he is said to know a lot. Both these passions are covered well in his paper.

After eight years of successful and liberal editorship, Preston made a significant mistake which to many reveals a weakness in his own and the *Guardian*'s character. This was, of course, the decision to return the memorandum on the deployment of cruise missiles written by the Secretary of Defence, Michael Heseltine, and leaked to the newspaper by a junior clerical officer. The paper fought to retain the document and thus protect whoever had supplied it, but after a rapid succession of court hearings Preston was ordered to hand it over, which he did in full knowledge that the security service would use it in an attempt to trace the paper's source.

Preston and his senior executives and lawyers were rattled by the government's evident determination. As a result they displayed a bewildering lack of concern for their source, the *Guardian*'s credibility and, in the face of such blatant official pressure, the standing of the press generally. Preston argued that there were two compelling reasons for obeying the court. In the dispute between Mr Eddie Shah, the proprietor of the *Stockport Messenger*, and the National Graphical Association, the courts had demonstrated their power to fine as wealthy and as bellicose an organisation as the N.G.A. into submission. The *Guardian* is owned by the Scott Trust and is largely supported by its sister paper the *Manchester Evening News*. The paper could not, they argued, have withstood successive penalties for contempt of court. Secondly, during the same dispute the *Guardian*, together with the rest of Fleet Street, had insisted that the N.G.A. should uphold the rule of law whatever the principles involved. If, then, in a matter of weeks the *Guardian* was to justify disobedience of the law in defence of another principle, Preston and his leader writers would have been open to accusations of inconsistency, not to mention hypocrisy.

Of course none of this public agony would have been necessary if the *Guardian* had had the sense to destroy the document in the first place. But given its existence, Preston should have placed above all other considerations confidentiality of its source and the necessity of resisting what Hugo Young writing in the *Sunday Times* called 'the thickening climate of official aggression against the press'.

During the court hearings I wondered how another editor would have handled the crisis; Harry Evans, the former editor of the *Sunday Times* and *Times*, for instance. Certainly he had his faults as an editor but they never extended to the pusillanimity and loss of nerve that Preston exhibited in December 1983. Had Preston mobilised his readers' opinion the way Evans had done during the court battle to publish the Crossman Diaries and the *Sunday Times*'s investigations into the Thalidomide scandal, the paper might just have got another result and certainly would have emerged from the affair with some integrity. It would have been dangerously expensive, true, and the *Guardian* leader writers would have looked a little silly, but it would not have been for the first time.

To be fair to Preston he was appalled by the whole business, particularly when Sarah Tisdall was sentenced to six months in prison. Still, he has nothing but the lack of his own conviction to blame.

THE MIRROR GROUP
Daily Mirror; Sunday Mirror; Sunday People

MIKE MOLLOY: EDITOR, *Daily Mirror*
Mike Molloy, the forty-four-year-old Editor of the *Daily Mirror*, must occasionally marvel at the ease with which he came to occupy one of the most prized jobs in popular journalism. His relatively humble back-ground in West London gives no clue either to his journalistic ability or to the ambition which was to propel him so swiftly to the top. He trained at the Ealing School of Art, where he exhibited a flair for draftsmanship and painting (examples of Molloy's artistic efforts are still occasionally accepted for the Royal Academy Summer Exhibition). In 1956 he

joined the layout department of the *Sunday Pictorial* and conceived a great love for newspapers. After a spell at the *Daily Sketch* he returned to the Mirror group in 1962 and eventually became editor of the ill-fated but ambitious *Mirror Magazine*. Unlike most editors who have risen from the subs' table Molloy has an instinctive respect for writers, a fact which has won him many friends among the journalists of the *Mirror*. In 1970 he became an Assistant Editor and in 1975, at the age of thirty-four, he was appointed editor.

Molloy's mild, even deferential manner belies his toughness and real concern for the quality of the *Daily Mirror*. His appearance is also deceptive. For while he looks like a sober and happily married professional he is frequently to be found at the centre of the rowdy gambling sessions held by his colleagues. Like Peter Preston of the *Guardian* Molloy is an excellent delegator; rather than pretending to any journalistic omniscience he prefers to use the skills and knowledge of his own staff.

During the nine years of his editorship Molloy's principal achievement has been to withstand the pressure to compete with the *Sun* and the *Daily Star* on their own terms. There are obviously areas in which he has been forced to compromise (the use of nudes, bingo promotions and exaggerated royal stories) but generally the paper still exhibits a desire to inform its readership. He believes that the greatest concession has been made in the packaging of the paper. At the time of the price-cutting war with the *Sun* he observed, 'I don't think our content has changed dramatically but the packaging has. We've become more competitive about our packaging because we didn't bother before. But you won't find that our political coverage has changed.'

The encouraging thing about the *Daily Mirror*, and one hopes it will not change under Clive Thornton, the new chairman of the Mirror Group, is that it does aspire to something other than selling more and more newspapers. Occasionally entire issues are given over to such subjects as nuclear weapons and the health service, while the daily 'package' includes intelligent writing from Joe Haines, Keith Waterhouse and Peter Tory, the editor of the *Mirror* Diary, who is a good deal more generous than his rivals. (But see Stop Press, p. 196.)

The most illuminating part of Mike Molloy's editorship during 1983 was his refusal to publish two very sensational stories. During the summer the *Mirror* was informed that Cecil Parkinson's former secretary Sara Keays was expecting his child. Although she was unforthcoming when the paper asked for an interview, it was throughout the autumn in a strong position to use the story. Molloy resisted the temptation. He displayed a similar distaste in December 1983 when his paper learned that the former ambassador to Washington, Peter Jay, had been living with his children's nanny and was suspected of being the father of her child.

Once the stories had broken elsewhere the *Mirror*, of course, did as much as any other newspaper to torment Parkinson and Jay. But his original instincts in both cases were right.

BOB EDWARDS: EDITOR, *Sunday Mirror*

When Bob Edwards was interviewed by the Mirror Group's *News* in 1975 he uttered this memorable remark: 'If I'd been a musician I'd have liked to have played in a stylish band like Tommy Dorsey's. The *Sunday Mirror* has that style.' Few could have hoped to capture the flavour of Mr Edwards and his newspaper more concisely.

Born in 1925, Edwards is the oldest tabloid newspaper editor. He went to Ranelagh, a direct grant grammar school near Bracknell; a fervent supporter of the Labour party, his first job was with the *Reading Mercury* as an office boy. After he brought in a rather good local story he was quickly made a reporter. In the spirit of postwar socialism he conceived the idea of starting up a local Labour newspaper in Reading and suggested it to the Labour politician Ian Mikardo. The paper never got off the ground, but Mikardo was impressed with Edwards and mentioned his name to Michael Foot. Edwards was soon installed at *Tribune*, which he edited from 1951 to 1954. In 1957 Lord Beaverbrook, a close friend of Michael Foot's, appointed him Deputy Editor of the *Sunday Express*, a paper which hardly reflected Edwards's politics, but which nevertheless represented enormous possibilities for a twenty-nine-year old journalist. Beaverbrook's confidence in him was expressed by a number of promotions which culminated in 1963 in the offer of the editorship of the *Daily Express*, then one of the prize jobs in Fleet Street. By all accounts his two years in the job were fraught. He was dismissed once and quickly reinstated and then finally dismissed again in 1965. The following year he took over at the *Sunday People* and in 1972 became Editor of the *Sunday Mirror*.

Edwards is generally considered to be a likeable man and a competent editor. His abilities were, however, called into question in the winter of 1980 when his paper published the story that Prince Charles had been joined on the Royal Train by Lady Diana Spencer. Unusually, Edwards reproduced a strong letter of refutation from the Queen's Press Secretary, Michael Shea, on the front page. Inside the same issue he reprinted a letter from himself to Shea which robustly defended the story but which failed to produce one piece of convincing evidence to support it. The *Daily Mail* took particular satisfaction in Edwards's predicament. During the *Daily Mail*'s embarrassment over the Leyland Bribes affair, Edwards had delivered a stinging rebuke to David English criticising him for allowing his strong dislike of the Labour Party to interfere with his judgement as an editor. English took the opportunity to attack Edwards, accusing him of 'nauseating hypocrisy'. And the *Sunday Times*, in the shape of Stephen Pile, decided that for a change Mr Edwards ought to be harassed and sent his assistant to ask him some impertinent questions.

The memory of the incident was clearly still with Edwards two years later when the *Sunday Mirror*'s crime reporter presented the paper with the story of Michael Fagan's break-in at Buckingham Palace. Although it was based on impeccable sources, the story was rejected as being too incredible. The next day it was used in the *Daily Express*.

RICHARD STOTT: EDITOR, *Sunday People*

Nicholas Lloyd's successor at the *Sunday People* is Richard Stott, a very talented investigator who led the enquiries into the disappearance of John Stonehouse and the behaviour of the football manager Don Revie.

He started his journalistic career with the Dartford News Agency, where he had the dubious pleasure of working with the current editor of the *Sun*, Kelvin Mackenzie. After ten years as a leading reporter with the *Daily Mirror* he decided that it was time for him to take an interest in the paper's direction. He applied for an executive position but was turned down by Mike Molloy. Rather than return to the newsroom, Stott resigned and announced that he would be working out his notice at home. This seems to have brought the *Daily Mirror* management to its senses and he was hastily appointed Features Editor in 1979. His abilities as an executive turned out to be really rather remarkable. In 1981 he became Assistant Editor in charge of features (more a pay rise than a promotion) and in 1982 he was put in overall charge of the paper's news and photographic operation. Such was his influence that when he came to leave the paper in 1984 many bemoaned his loss. There is, perhaps, in Stott a little naiveté. When he took over he told the Mirror Group's house magazine: 'In the past the paper has tended to buy in a lot of stuff but this is no longer our policy. We certainly won't be spending a great deal of money in that direction.' Commendable though this sentiment may be, he is now competing directly with Nicholas Lloyd, who *will* use the chequebook to win readers.

NEWS INTERNATIONAL
News of the World; Sun; The Times; Sunday Times

RUPERT MURDOCH: PROPRIETOR

When Rupert Murdoch was attempting to take over the *New York Daily News*, which was owned by the *Chicago Tribune*, the company gave its reply in the way that it felt Mr Murdoch would best understand. The front page of the *News* was taken up with the banner headline: TRIB TO RUPERT: DROP DEAD. In the unlikely event of Murdoch following this instruction, one wonders how long his empire of newspapers, TV interests and publishing and transport concerns would take to follow him. For it is an unnerving fact of life for the many thousands of people that he employs across three continents that their future security largely depends on the continuing good health of Rupert Keith Murdoch.

He was born in 1931 to Sir Keith Murdoch, the forty-five-year-old publisher of the *Brisbane Courier-Mail* and the *Adelaide News*. Sir Keith, a man of strong-willed Scottish ancestry, had married late in life, having already established himself as a great reporter in the First World War and a very competent editor afterwards. The age of his father is generally considered to be one of the decisive influences in Rupert's formative years. Although the family was happy and secure, Sir Keith and Rupert did not have the closest of relationships. Sir Keith had strong views on the sort of qualities it would take to inherit a newspaper business and set about toughening his young son with a disciplinarian education at Geelong Grammar School, supported in the holidays by a strict régime which involved the young Rupert sleeping in the garden shed.

He came into his father's business a lot earlier than either of them expected. At the age of twenty he inherited the *Adelaide News* (his mother sold the Brisbane paper), having just emerged from Oxford University, where he had taken a degree in Politics, Philosophy and Economics. At this stage people remember him as a likable sort of chap. Alexander Chancellor, the former editor of the *Spectator*, recalled the young Murdoch: 'He used often to visit us in Hertfordshire, usually turning up on a motorcycle, and everyone liked him. He was bright, intelligent, jolly and straightforward. His hero at the time was Asa Briggs' (then an Oxford don and now Lord Briggs).

When Murdoch arrived in Adelaide to lay claim to his inheritance, he had had very little journalistic experience – just a few months as junior sub-editor on Beaverbrook's *Daily Express*. By all accounts his first years as a proprietor were characterised by a willingness to learn every aspect of the newspaper business and by a politeness to his subordinates. Gradually, however, the features which have shaped his career began to appear. He started to take a close interest in the actual production of the paper, meddling with headlines and suggesting different presentation of news items. In 1959, at the age of twenty-eight, he fired Rohan Rivett, editor of the *Adelaide News* and his friend, and he began negotiating his first takeover, that of the Australian *Daily*

Mirror. The next decade was spent building a strong financial platform from which to launch his move to Fleet Street, which in Murdoch's eyes was still the repository of the best journalistic skills in the world. The opportunity came in 1969 when the feuding Carr family decided to put the *News of the World* on the market. After a long, acrimonious struggle against that other outsider, the Czech-born publisher Robert Maxwell, Murdoch succeeded. He set about looking for a paper to take up the spare printing capacity of the *News of the World*, whose presses lay idle from one Saturday night to the next. The Daily Mirror Group, under Hugh Cudlipp, had decided to dispose of the *Sun*, on the grounds that I.P.C. could no longer afford the huge losses the paper had incurred in its brief life. Soon after Murdoch had occupied his offices at Bouverie Street he published the memoirs of Christine Keeler, one of the call-girls in the Profumo affair. Despite its prurient interest in such high-class scandal, the British establishment was outraged that Murdoch, a cocksure outsider, was raking over this embarrassing episode in the nation's recent history. Murdoch was attacked in every quarter and during the row decided to give his view of the story in a television interview with David Frost. It turned out to be one of the most humiliating experiences of his career. He was never again to lay himself open to attack and many believe that famous exchange caused Murdoch to turn to America, although the bungled kidnap and murder of the wife of Alex McKay, a *News of the World* executive, was a contributing factor. Anna Murdoch was the intended target.

Within months of his arrival in 1973 Murdoch had bought three profitable little titles in San Antonio, Texas. The expansion that followed was phenomenal. He founded the *National Star* to compete with the odious *National Enquirer*; he bought the *New York Post* and, after a series of notorious manoeuvres against his friend Clay Felker, *New York* magazine.

Murdoch seemed to be driven by an insatiable acquisitiveness, which frightened as much as scandalised the rather staid and complacent world of American journalism. The *Village Voice* soon fell into his hands, despite its leftward tendencies, and more recently the pres-tigious *Chicago Sun-Times* and *Boston Herald*. Each of these acquisitions was followed by a rapid exodus of journalists denouncing their new proprietor as a vandaliser of great institutions. Murdoch appears to have been remarkably unaffected and turned his attention back to Britain, where the Thomson Organisation had finally indicated that the £40 million losses incurred during the shutdown of *The Times* and *Sunday Times* was the last straw. The events that followed are chronicled at length in Harold Evans's book *Good Times, Bad Times*, but here is one paragraph which sums up the general theme:

> He guaranteed that editors would have control of the political policy of their newspapers; that they would have freedom within fixed annual budgets; that editors would not be subject to instruction from either the proprietor or management on the selection and balance of news and opinion; and that any future sale of the titles would require agreement of a majority of independent national directors. In my years as Editor of *The Times*, Murdoch broke all those guarantees. He put his point of view very simply to the Home Editor of *The Times*, Fred Emery . . . 'I give instructions to my editors all round the world, why shouldn't I in London?' He was reminded of the undertakings to the Secretary of State. 'They're not worth the paper they're written on,' replied Murdoch.

The purchase of these two great newspapers and the highbrow periodicals which went with them was the summit of Murdoch's achievement so far. But as if he believed that old adage that as soon as an empire ceases to expand it begins to collapse, Murdoch was on the move again. In 1983 he started to make some distinctly aggressive overtures to Warner Brothers, the huge American communications conglomerate. The *Daily Telegraph* was sufficiently awed by this news to break it in the headline, MURDOCH ON THE WAY TO WORLD LEADERSHIP. While of course it referred to Murdoch's near pre-eminence in the world of communications, it nicely captures the megalomania many have attributed to Murdoch.

Certainly Murdoch has enjoyed exercising the power that his papers have brought him. In Australia he played a crucial role in the electoral contest between Malcolm Fraser and Gough Whitlam. As Whitlam said, 'Anyone who works for his papers knows how odious Mr Murdoch's control is. Some of his employees have come round Australia with me and they are finding it very hard to get their stories published.' In Britain Murdoch came down heavily on the side of Mrs Thatcher. Coincidentally, and at much the same time, Larry Lamb seems to have undergone a similar conversion. In America Murdoch has at various times supported Ed Koch for the mayoral office in New York and opposed Jimmy Carter. Even so there are signs that Murdoch does not enjoy political brokerage as much as, say, Beaverbrook or Northcliffe did. In such interviews as he has given on the subject of politics he always seems to have pretty basic views, and commentators have been frequently struck by his lack of subtlety and understanding.

What else, then, can have driven Murdoch these past three decades? Is it simply a wholesome love of the newspaper industry? Certainly he enjoys a night seeing the last edition to bed as much as he relishes a takeover battle, but there is little evidence that he has any strong affection for journalists or their product. If anything, he has displayed a consistent contempt for 'journos', as he calls them, particularly the sort of journo who takes his profession seriously and makes important statements about duty to democracy. As to the quality of his newspapers, his only criterion seems to be commercial appeal.

Perhaps it is prestige which he has been after all these years? Unlikely. He does not lay great stress on the views of others, particularly those who feel their views should be taken into account. Although he has recently accepted the Companion Order of Australia, he has several times turned down offers of a knighthood in Britain. Unlike rather more sensitive press barons, he has never resorted to the libel laws to defend himself.

Both Harold Evans and Michael Leapman, Murdoch's biographer, implicitly make the judgment that Murdoch is indeed a megalomaniac, simply concerned with the acquisition of more and more power. This may be partly true, but the evidence also points to a personality which is absorbed by risk and challenge and the pleasure of upsetting conventional wisdom. The adjectives which come to mind are ruthless, impulsive, unprincipled and above all cunning.

NICHOLAS LLOYD: EDITOR, *News of the World*

Nick Lloyd's recent career is as good an argument for chequebook journalism as you are likely to find. During the eighteen months of his editorship of the *Sunday People* he is estimated to have spent between £1,000,000 and £1,500,000 on the purchase of stories, features and serialisations. By the time he came to leave the *People* in January 1984 he had put on 40,000 copies. These had largely been attracted away from Rupert Murdoch's *News of the World*, which had lost nearly 200,000 copies in the same period. There was really only one sensible course open to Murdoch: to dismiss Derek Jameson, convert the paper to a tabloid format and bring in Lloyd. He promptly did all three and already the paper is regaining readers.

On the face of it Nicholas Lloyd would seem to be an unlikely editor of a popular newspaper; his early career gives no hint that he would be the man that Murdoch chose to take the *News of the World* down market. Born into a comfortable middle-class home in 1942, Lloyd was a bright child who was eventually to win a place to study history at St Edmund's Hall, Oxford. At the age of twenty-two he became a reporter for the *Daily Mail* and in 1966 joined the golden intake of the *Sunday Times*, where he served as Education Correspondent and, later as Deputy News Editor under Harry Evans. Lloyd's first break in popular journalism came in 1968 when he was chosen by Larry Lamb as the News Editor of the relaunched *Sun*. He was to spend twelve years with Murdoch's organisation, in which he became Assistant Editor of the *News of the World* and then Assistant Editor at the *Sun*. In 1980 the *Sunday Mirror*'s editor Bob Edwards persuaded Lloyd to defect from News International. There was a very attractive salary and a strong hint that the deputy editorship of the *Sunday Mirror* would be followed by the editorship of the *Sunday People*. He became editor in 1982.

Lloyd's time at the *Sunday People* is remembered with a mixture of admiration and astonishment. One of his first acts was to spend a considerable sum on the refurbishment of his office. This was shortly followed by the employment of the attractive and intelligent Eve Pollard in a senior position. She also happens to be the second Mrs Lloyd. One member of the staff recalls: 'It was certainly a surprising decision but we were so taken aback by the amount of money Lloyd was spending on buying-in material that everyone soon forgot about it. Much of it was spent outbidding the rival Sunday newspapers, but there was also a good deal of unnecessary expenditure. If he had had his way, he would have filled the paper with nothing but tits and stories about *Coronation Street*. He is the essence of a popular newspaper editor.'

In this he has much in common with David Montgomery, who he met on the *Sunday Mirror*. Montgomery's chief ability is to make the most of material by the use of bold layouts and screeching headlines. Lloyd employed him at the *Sunday People* and then, with Murdoch's blessing, took him to the *News of the World*. Students of the popular press credit much of Lloyd's initial success at the *News of the World* to Montgomery.

DEREK JAMESON: FORMER EDITOR, *News of the World*
Derek Jameson was born within the smell of Hackney marshes in 1930 to an Irish mother and a Jewish father who disappeared shortly after he was conceived. He was brought up in poor circumstances and received an education of sorts at Hackney Elementary School. He had every opportunity to follow a profitable career in crime; however, he also discovered that he had a talent for English. He entered a national competition by writing an essay on the Red Cross and won the first prize of a five-pound book token. Today, he admits that he copied most of his entry from a pamphlet in the local library. However, his success seems to have convinced him that journalism might pay. He started as a street messenger at the Reuters News Agency and, after considerable self-education, progressed first to a reporter's desk and later to the position of chief sub-editor. After an uneventful national service he went to the *Daily Express* under Bob Edwards and then followed him to the *Sunday Mirror*. Jameson was to make his name as the Northern Editor of the *Daily Mirror* when it was fighting for circulation with the *Sun*.

Jameson's career might have taken an altogether different course had he accepted the offer of a friend who wanted to publish a magazine for men. The friend, who was then in the dry-cleaning business, was Bob Guccione, now the multi-millionaire publisher of *Penthouse*. Still, while

Jameson lost a fortune, there are many who would agree that he has done as much as Mr Guccione in the service of soft pornography. When asked by the *Observer* what the *Daily Star* would be like under his editorship he replied, 'Well, it's going to be tits, bums, Q.P.R. and roll your own fags.' Pressed on the number of nipples the *Star* planned to publish each day he said that it would not have eight to every two in the *Sun*, but that there would be a regular supply of good-quality nipples.

Nudity of late has played a large part in Jameson's life. In the spring of 1984 he was to be found in the High Court in London, defending his reputations against the B.B.C. radio programme *Stop the Week*, which had described him as an 'East End boy made bad' and his style of journalism as 'All the nudes fit to print and the news printed to fit.' The exchanges between Jameson, who had unwisely brought the libel action, and the Counsel for the B.B.C. must be among the most hilarious ever to have been heard in the law courts. For his part, Jameson tried to prove that 'honesty and integrity' still existed in the tabloid press while the B.B.C. resurrected a number of stories from the *Daily Star*'s files to show that under Mr Jameson the paper really *was* only interested in 'tits, bums, Q.P.R. and roll your own fags.' The proceedings developed into a trial of the tastes and ethics of popular newspaper editors and so it was not surprising that the jury found in favour of the B.B.C. and awarded it legal costs, a financial blow from which Jameson has still not recovered.

His determination to vindicate himself is measure of his pride, but more so of his sensitivity. He said in 1975 while still with the *Daily Mirror*, 'My staff think I'm a bland character with a ruthless streak. I'm not like that at all. I have a great regard for human dignity and I'm sensitive to personal criticism.' Throughout his career he has proved incapable of ignoring attacks. When Auberon Waugh, writing in the *Spectator*, turned his attention to the editorship of the *Daily Express*, Jameson made the mistake of replying to Waugh in print. Here is part of Waugh's attack:

> It is a crude and tasteless thing to mock a man for his accent unless it is upper class, but to ignore Jameson's cockney would be more insulting, like ignoring a man who arrives at a party wearing

a false nose. In appointing him, Matthews plainly intended to make a statement about something.

Waugh went on to mock Jameson's statement of policy at the *Express*: 'Us four oz oim concerned ve *Daily Express* will never carry nippos.'

The next week Jameson completed Waugh's satisfaction by writing:

> Presumably these insults rest on the fact that I am from the East End, grew up in poverty and left school at fourteen. Would you believe that there are people from the working class who can read and write?

All of this ignores Jameson's quite remarkable abilities as a popular journalist. His move from the *Mirror* to the *Daily Express*, after a rather boastful application to Lord Matthews, was marked by a rise in circulation and some genuinely fresh ideas. Jameson has a very real flair for newspaper design and an instinct for what interests his readers. However, when he was finally summoned by Murdoch to edit the *News of the World*, he seems to have suffered a loss of inspiration which did little to stop the last popular broadsheet from losing circulation. Murdoch's patience ran out at the end of 1983 and Jameson was replaced by Nick Lloyd, the former editor of the *Sunday People*.

One hopes that Jameson finds himself another niche, although it seems unlikely that he will edit a fourth national newspaper.

KELVIN MACKENZIE: EDITOR, the *Sun*

As a teenager Kelvin MacKenzie acquired the sort of qualification necessary to reach the editor's chair of the *Sun*: One o-level. There is some doubt as to the subject of his single academic success, but the majority of opinion tends to the view that it cannot have been English. He was born on October 22, 1946, in South London. Although Mr MacKenzie has done his level best to affect a working-class manner he was in fact brought up in the bosom of the bourgeoisie. His father was a successful journalist in a group of South London newspapers and Kelvin, together with his brothers Drew and Craig, was educated at Alleyn's School, Dulwich, a private school which has a reasonably good academic record. One of MacKenzie's school acquaintances remembers him thus: 'He was bad at everything. He shouted and swore the loudest. He was a bully.' By all accounts he has changed little since then. His first job was engineered by his father. He chose sub-editing rather than reporting as the skill that would advance him into Fleet Street. In 1973 he became a junior sub-editor under Larry Lamb at the *Sun* and by 1976 he had risen to Assistant Night Editor. After a two year spell as Managing Editor of the *New York Post*, he returned to the *Sun* as Night Editor in 1980. The following year he briefly worked at the *Daily Express* but was wooed back to Bouverie Street following Lamb's departure to Australia.

MacKenzie's three-year editorship has been characterised by a blind patriotism, a contempt for his readers' intelligence and an unquestioning belief in the infallibility of Mrs Thatcher. He first came to public attention during the Falklands war when, as 'The Paper That Supports Our Boys', the *Sun* ran some bloodthirsty headlines (the sinking of the *Belgrano* was headlined GOTCHA!) and extraordinarily inaccurate stories (the paper announced the recapture of the island of South Georgia well before it had actually happened). The war coverage was a signal that something rather remarkable was happening at the *Sun*. MacKenzie's carelessness even began to shock journalists on rival newspapers. What is, perhaps, most extraordinary about MacKenzie is that he remains utterly unaffected by the very serious condemnation of the Press Council and the frequent exposure by other newspapers. He has isolated himself with a crude set of editorial values which chiefly revolve round selling more and more of Mr Murdoch's papers. This isolation has been compounded by a refusal to give interviews to television or to other journalists. His staff suspect that this may in part be due to his inability to talk without punctuating most phrases with swearwords.

In Bouverie Street, the tubby figure of the *Sun* Editor is nevertheless held in some awe. He can be quite ruthless in his dealings with his staff. Some have found that life under MacKenzie is simply too unpleasant and have given up their very large salaries for more peaceful surroundings elsewhere. Last year MacKenzie demoted the paper's experienced political editor, Walter Terry, to an ordinary reporter's job; because he disagreed with the way in which Terry presented politics. (Happily the

N.U.J. interceded and Mr Terry left with a cheque for £80,000.) MacKenzie is also fond of sending abusive memos to his staff. One which recently circulated read:

I am disgusted at the length of your lunch hours. Two hour breaks do not do this newspaper, this country or yourselves a favour. It is no wonder that Britain is rapidly turning into a third world country.

He may have a point about the length of journalists' lunch breaks, but it is a measure of the fantastic notions that spin through his mind that he believes that a *Sun* reporter's extra hour in the pub is contributing to the decline of the nation (in fact, one might suggest that the longer the reporters remain away from their typewriters, the better it is for all of us).

There is a temptation to indulge his erratic behaviour and outrageous journalism by seeing him as a buffoon. But the reality of Mr MacKenzie is much more serious: even the Soaraway *Sun* has a duty to truth as well as entertainment.

CHARLES DOUGLAS-HOME: EDITOR, *The Times*

If Derek Jameson is the epitome of a popular newspaper editor, Charles Cospatrick Douglas-Home is everything that an Editor of *The Times* ought to be. He was a King's Scholar at Eton, he was commissioned into the Royal Scots Greys, he served as ADC to the Governor of Kenya, Sir Evelyn Baring, and is the nephew of a former Conservative Prime Minister; he has the passions and pastimes of the landed gentry; the retiring manner, clipped speech, and disdain for clothes that characterise patrician blood.

Professionally he always seemed destined for New Printing House Square, although he started his career as a local reporter for the *Daily Express* in Scotland. He moved to cover Defence and Politics for the paper in London, but at the age of twenty-seven was chosen to succeed Lord Chalfont as the *Times* Defence Correspondent. In 1967 he covered the Six-Day War and established a reputation for himself which was further enhanced by books on the Middle East, Rommel and British defence. He was the sort of young man who appealed to William

Rees-Mogg, the then editor, who is no plebeian himself. Douglas-Home was advanced to Features Editor and then Home Editor, an important position on the paper. There is an effortless quality about his rise which belies a remarkable ambition. When it comes down to it, Mr Douglas-Home is attracted by power as much as, say, Sir David English or Sir Larry Lamb. This was one of the minor themes of Harry Evans's book *Good Times, Bad Times*, and though Evans occasionally makes factual errors in the record of his fifteen years with the *Sunday Times* and *Times*, he presents overwhelming evidence to support this view.

Having failed to acquire Hugo Young, the distinguished Political Editor of the *Sunday Times*, as his deputy, Evans was encouraged by the outgoing William Rees-Mogg to take on Douglas-Home, an appointment that neither seemed particularly enthusiastic about. Evans portrays Douglas-Home at this stage as deferring to his judgment, complimenting him on the paper and urging him to stand up for the decency and integrity that *The Times* had always represented. He was privately critical of Murdoch, describing him as 'Jaws II', 'a wrecker of institutions', and 'a monster'. As Evans's relationship with Murdoch deteriorated and the paper began to attract criticism from outside, notably from Murdoch's friend Paul Johnson, Douglas-Home quietly transferred his allegiance to the old-guard *Times* people, who were bitter with Evans over changes in the paper and the appointment of cronies from the *Sunday Times*. Evans does not appear to have appreciated it at the time, but Douglas-Home was slowly working to become his heir apparent. In the last month of Evans's editorship Murdoch sent for Douglas-Home and offered him the chair. There then followed the most unseemly episode in the paper's distinguished history. Evans's staff rebelled and some even leaked private memoranda to the national press; his secretary appears to have informed on him and Murdoch sent a number of menacing lieutenants to remove him from the post. All the while Charles Douglas-Home, the Editor Designate, remained in the background affecting a statesmanlike contempt for the whole unpleasant business. However, a rumour that Larry Lamb might be appointed instead of himself made him break cover and, in an astonishing phone call to Evans, he is reported as saying, 'You little fucker, I'll come in there and wring your neck. You've told people Larry Lamb will be the next editor, you bastard you.'

The words used by Douglas-Home may not have been exactly as recorded by Evans, but he has never denied them in public, so we may assume that a conversation on these lines took place. Evans, also, may not be entirely without fault in the exchange, for his close friends believe that it was quite in character for him to spread a rumour that Douglas-Home might yet have the job wrenched from him. Whatever the facts of the matter, it seems that Douglas-Home did not behave in the gentlemanly way that one might expect.

In the middle seventies *Private Eye* revealed that when Douglas-Home was Home Editor he compiled a dossier on the private lives of his staff in which he discussed people's social background ('he's not a gentleman'), their love-lives ('chaotic love-life affects his work'), and their state of mind. After strong protest by the union, Douglas-Home was forced to apologise and later gave an undertaking that he would destroy the records.

As a journalist, Douglas-Home is competent but has none of the enthusiasm of Evans. His value to Murdoch is that he is more open to suggestions and more at one with his political views. *The Times* itself has changed considerably since the days of William Rees-Mogg. Its critics say that it is no longer the paper of record and that it does not carry the weight it once did. The leader comments are considered to be less sound intellectually. Many of the changes, particularly in presentation and news values, were brought about during Evans's term; Douglas-Home, although laid up for long periods with a serious back complaint, has introduced a lively but sometimes vacuous features spread and improved the sports coverage.

FRANK GILES: EDITOR EMERITUS, *Sunday Times*
ANDREW NEIL: EDITOR, *Sunday Times*

Frank Giles was born in 1919 into a well-to-do family. He was educated at Wellington College, a public school of strong military traditions of which he is now a governor. Giles, by all accounts an elegant young man, displayed an academic turn of mind rather than any inclination to enter the neighbouring Sandhurst. He won a history scholarship to Brasenose College, Oxford, where he performed with competence rather than flair. With relative ease he took his first job in the diplomatic world, serving as ADC to the Governor of Bermuda. After the war he was for a time the private secretary to Ernest Bevin, then Foreign Secretary. In manner, temperament and credentials, Giles seemed ideally suited to a lifelong career in British embassies; but he appears to have decided that his real vocation lay in journalism and joined the foreign staff of *The Times* as a member of the Paris Bureau. After a period in Rome, he returned to Paris as chief correspondent. He became foreign editor of the *Sunday Times* in 1961, long before the then editor brought the bustling, enthusiastic figure of Harold Evans from the north. Evans's arrival effectively eclipsed Giles's hopes for the editorship, but he was content to serve as a loyal if somewhat cautious deputy to Evans, putting the brake on some of the latter's more extravagant ideas. By the time the post was offered to him by the new proprietor of Times Newspapers, Rupert Murdoch, Giles was known by his colleagues to be contemplating a comfortable retirement with his vivacious wife, Lady Kitty, the daughter of the 9th Earl De La Warr, pursuing his interests of Burgundy and opera.

Giles was clearly only ever a caretaker. His main priority was to retain the integrity that the *Sunday Times* possessed under Lord Thomson and to preserve the traditions of fine writing and exposure that Evans had fostered. If anything Giles tried too hard, with the result that the paper became less and less adventurous and, some would say, even moribund under his editorship. While the structure of the paper had changed little – neither the staff nor its appearance had been radically altered – the drive had gone with Harry Evans. To be fair to Giles, his two-year term was considerably handicapped by Murdoch's insistence on savage cuts in the paper's budget, which were executed by the former head of Reuters, Gerald Long. There was also a succession of confrontations with the unions and Murdoch threatened at regular intervals to close down the paper. This had the effect of diverting his attention from the main business in hand and demoralising his staff. While they were dissatisfied with his cautious, respectful approach to the establishment, thought by many to have been acquired during his early days in the diplomatic service, the senior executives stayed in the belief that he was an effective buffer between the marauding Murdoch and themselves.

Two months after the paper's humiliating endorsement of the Hitler Diaries, a project which had been forced on Giles by Murdoch, he announced at the weekly editorial conference that he was retiring. He was to be replaced by Andrew Neil, of whom he knew very little. Murdoch had met Neil, the then thirty-four-year-old Home Editor of the *Economist*, while investigating the possibilities of cable TV. Neil had joined a company, National Economic Research Associates, to advise on the effects it would have on traditional broadcasting. He recalls the turn that these meetings took: 'He started to say to me, "What do you think of the *Sunday Times*?" I gave my opinions about it and after I saw him for about the fifth time we were talking more about the *Sunday Times* and less about satellites.'

Following the announcement Giles took Neil to lunch at his club. Legend has it that Giles interrupted the conversation to talk to the Archbishop of Canterbury, whom he had spotted at another table. The exchange was brief and courteous. Giles returned to Neil and declared that that was the sort of person you could say 'Good morning' to once you were editor of the *Sunday Times*.

It is an indication of Neil's radically different background and personality that he was not the slightest bit impressed by the possibility of hobnobbing with the Archbishop. He was born in Paisley in 1949. He was educated at Paisley Grammar school and Glasgow University and left in 1971 with a reasonable degree in Politics and Economics. Neil's twenties were marked by an intense desire to get on, which first displayed itself in frenetic activity for the Conservative party and, later, as the political advisor to a key figure in the Heath government, Peter Walker. He joined the *Economist* in 1973, where he served as Ulster correspondent, Labour Editor and the magazine's correspondent in America. He became Home Editor in 1982. From each of these specialist jobs he retained what appears to be an encyclopaedic knowledge of the area he covered. He is particularly enamoured of America, and generally holds the view that everything that happens there is bigger, better and ultimately more interesting than anywhere else. He is also fascinated by the possibilities of new technology or, as he calls it, the Sunrise Industries.

In October 1983 Giles was elevated to the position of Editor Emeritus, a new and unusually generous sinecure in which he retained a number of attractive perks, while Neil moved into the editor's office. He brought with him sweeping plans for change which emphasised the coverage of new technology and the promotion of youth. These largely offended the old guard of the *Sunday Times*, many of whom, although not particularly old, had been with the paper since their mid-twenties. Among those who left, some with considerable redundancy payments, were Hugo Young, Political Editor, Peter Calvocoressi, Foreign Writer, John Wale, Religious Affairs Correspondent, Christopher Hurd, Editor of Insight, Stephen Fay, Washington Correspondent, and leading feature writers Elaine Potter, Colin Simpson and Peter Gillman. The exodus, which lasted until the spring of 1984, received unfavourable publicity, particularly at the *New Statesman*, where Peter Kellner wrote:

> Part of the paper's strength over the past twenty years has been that of a double role: as both member and critic of the establishment, its criticisms had impact precisely because it was not a lefty paper. Rather, it was one that, when occasions demanded, possessed the determination, the journalistic resources to penetrate the establishment's tawdry mask. Under Rupert Murdoch and Neil, the determination has gone, the resources have been diverted and much of the talent has left.

Kellner, of course, is an old *Sunday Times* man who tends towards the notion that nothing was quite so grand in British journalism as the paper under the first ten years of Harold Evans's editorship. The remarks irritated Neil, particularly as he viewed himself as being in the tradition of Harry Evans rather than Frank Giles. The changes have indeed been far-reaching. There is, for instance, far less investigative journalism, if only because the number of staff available for long projects is now small. It has been replaced by a number of sections which have compartmentalised the paper even more than under Evans and Giles. Neil has taken a much firmer political line than his two predecessors, especially in the area of privatisation, economics and industrial relations. He now writes the majority of leaders for the paper, having done away with much of the discussion which preceded the *Sunday Times* taking a view. He also has little reserve in changing journalists' copy and lecturing them on use of the hyphen and semi-colon. Those that have stayed have found that they have a mixed attitude to him. While he is personable to talk to they find his unmovable political convictions, his enormous self-confidence and his uncomplicated view of issues exasperating. Many of his critics have been confounded by the rise in circulation since he took over, especially as it is generally agreed that the product has not been improved.

Neil is said to be realistic about the life-span of editors under Murdoch, but has so far got on with him well. The paper has become more serious but less informed, more definite but less comprehending, more flashy but less stylish.

LONRHO
Observer

TINY ROWLAND: PROPRIETOR

It is difficult to imagine a proprietor less interested in the practice of journalism and the running of newspapers than Tiny Rowland. His purchase of the distinguished repository of liberality and fair-mindedness was neither motivated by desire for domestic prestige nor, oddly for Rowland, by dreams of large profits (the *Observer* was losing £4 million when he bought it). His only aim, as he told his old ally Daniel K. Ludwig, the American multi-millionaire, was to buy the voice which carried so much weight with the African statesmen that Lonrho, Rowland's conglomerate of mining, trading and transport interests, depended upon.

When the deal was announced it was Rowland's African interests which alarmed the *Observer* most of all. In the previous ten or twelve years it had done more than any paper to expose Rowland's unorthodox dealings in the continent, particularly his highly successful operation to carry on trading with the rebel régime in Rhodesia during sanctions. On the home front, barely a month passed without the paper giving extensive and unflattering coverage to Lonrho's boardroom disputes, investigation by the Department of Trade and Industry and its raids on the stock market. At the very moment that Tiny Rowland bought the paper from the Texas oil millionaire, Robert O. Anderson, the paper was campaigning against his aggressive bid for Harrods. The weekend before the deal was announced the city writer John David advised shareholders in Harrods 'how to beat off Tiny'. (Rowland responded by cancelling his company's advertising in the paper.)

Rowland's strength comes from the lack of any classifiable background. He has never been forthcoming about his private life, but it is known that he was born to a German father, named Furhop, and an English mother in India in 1917. He came to Britain shortly before the Second World War, changed his name and enlisted in the Medical Corps. He was discharged in 1942 as a corporal. He then disappeared into a succession of odd jobs, one of which appears to have had something to do with the manufacture of refrigeration equipment, but he denies the persistent myth that he started out as a railway porter at Paddington. At some point he emigrated to Rhodesia and quickly accumulated the money to buy two farms. For everything he has done since, a conventional British background, with its inherent rigidity of thought and respect for tradition, would have been a severe impediment. Rowland's success is based on the quick opportunism of the old-style capitalist adventurer. He has had the nerve to follow his instincts and the tenacity of someone who was born with little.

When the old colonial powers began to withdraw from Africa in the late 1950s and 1960s he was well placed to deal with the new independent governments. The banking establishment often shied away from Rowland's schemes but he usually got backing from somewhere on the strength of his obvious good relations with figures like Kenneth Kaunda and Julius Nyerere. In 1961 Rowland met Angus Ogilvy in Rhodesia and suggested a deal in which London Rhodesia, then an unsuccessful enterprise owned by Ogilvy's bank, should buy his business while he took over the management of the whole company, which was later to be re-named Lonrho. An incredible expansion followed, including the purchase of mining rights, a railway and newspapers in Zambia, Kenya, Tanzania and Uganda. Donald Trelford, the editor of the *Observer*, and his well-known African correspondent Colin Legum were to allege that Rowland used these newspapers to further his business interests and that he had no respect for editorial independence. Surprisingly this does not seem to have been the case. True, Rowland took care not to offend local régimes, but on the whole he seems to have exhibited a startling lack of interest in the everyday affairs of his papers.

If Rowland has made one mistake in his business life it has been to dismiss the conventions and institutions of Britain as easily as he would those of a newly formed African state. In 1973 Rowland's high-handed behaviour in Lonrho gave rise to a bitter struggle among Lonrho's shareholders which resulted in a long Department of Trade investigation into his handling of company funds. A lesser man would simply have resigned and waited for the Department to bring in its damaging report. Not Rowland. He used his famous charm and promise of profits to persuade the majority of Lonrho shareholders to support him. With this mandate he followed his instinct to the Middle East where he made a succession of profitable deals with the newly enriched Arabs. Three years later, when the Department of Trade and Industry eventually produced its report, Rowland launched a pre-emptive strike on his critics by inveighing against them in a stream of letters from his lawyers. Both he and Angus Ogilvy were criticised but it had little real effect on Tiny Rowland's business dealings.

In the light of Rowland's extraordinarily controversial career, it is not difficult to see why Donald Trelford and his colleagues at the *Observer* feared for the paper's integrity in 1981. Even if he took no direct action to influence the content of the newspaper, the mere fact of his ownership would mean that large areas of business and foreign reporting were out of bounds to the paper. In the last few years this has certainly been the case, and mentions of Rowland's interests or employees have been tactfully removed from the paper, for instance when the *Observer*'s Diarist Peter Hillmore tried to write about Edward du Cann, an old associate of Rowland's. Of late Rowland has been showing signs of exasperation with the journalists and the unions on the paper and in 1983 mentioned that he would happily sell up if he got the right price.

DONALD TRELFORD: EDITOR, *Observer*

Musing on his failure to buy the *Observer*, Rupert Murdoch said at a lunch of Times Newspapers executives, 'The biggest mistake I made was underestimating Donald Trelford. We had a meeting and then he went off and organised the opposition.' It is the highest compliment that Murdoch, a man who is rarely outwitted by editors, let alone editors of liberal-minded newspapers palpably on the brink of crisis, could pay. It is also an accurate account of events.

Trelford, the only editor in Fleet Street to be elected by a true poll of his paper's staff, had been spoilt by the benevolent rule of the last of the owner-editors, David Astor. When Astor announced that he could no longer subsidise the paper from within his personal fortune, the paper's trustees started hunting around for likely buyers. Lord Goodman approached Rupert Murdoch, who had his reservations but was prepared to listen. Trelford was dispatched on a secret visit to America with a view to talking to Murdoch and gaining certain guarantees. He returned to Britain convinced that the *Observer* should not be owned by the proprietor of the *Sun* and the *News of the World*. Somehow, and here one must suspect Trelford, details of the meeting with Murdoch reached the press, giving Trelford the opportunity to address his journalists and begin to 'organise the opposition'. Murdoch was outraged and withdrew with the following statement: 'In view of the breach of confidence that has taken place, together with the deliberate and orchestrated attempt to build this into a controversy, News International is no longer interested.'

Trelford's background gives no clue to his deft political skills and quiet opportunism. After Cambridge and National Service in the R.A.F., he trained as a journalist in Sheffield. By his twenty-fifth birthday he was editor of the *Nyasaland Times*. He ran the paper during the crucial period immediately before and after independence, acquiring along the way the sort of credentials that would appeal to David Astor. He returned to Britain in 1966 and moved swiftly up the *Observer* hierarchy to become Astor's deputy. In appearance he is short, neat and fastidious. He has a friendly and fluent manner and displays an apparent interest in the well-being of his colleagues.

The vacuum created by Murdoch's withdrawal was filled by Robert O. Anderson, the head of Atlantic Richfield, whose benevolence and generosity of spirit contrasted in every way with Murdoch's character. Here, then, was the perfect proprietor for the *Observer*; he had little interest in the British media and showed no inclination to interfere with the paper's policy. The relationship started perfectly, but after a while the *Observer*'s ways began to irritate him. He was, for instance, a strong admirer of Mrs Thatcher, and saw no sense in the *Observer*'s decision to back Jim Callaghan in the 1979 General Election. He grew tired of the *Observer*'s continual losses and was frustrated by the print unions' refusal to accept the new technology that was second nature to the American newspaper industry. The final irritant proved to be a minor one. The *Observer* journalist Kenneth Harris had originally introduced Anderson to the *Observer* and had been rewarded by a place on the board. Somewhat typically, this had caused a great deal of envy and malice among his colleagues, who felt that he had been promoted beyond his station. The paper's columnist Conor Cruise O'Brien even attacked Harris in a piece of coded vitriol printed in the *Observer*. There was, therefore, some considerable resentment when Atlantic Richfield suggested that Harris should be made vice-chairman of the *Observer* board. The board rejected the idea; on the same day Anderson agreed to sell the paper to Tiny Rowland.

Throughout the months of manoeuvring against Murdoch, the *Observer* Board and even Anderson, Trelford had only been limbering up for the really big battle of his career. Against Tiny Rowland he deployed every weapon he could muster. As I have already said, Trelford and his staff were most alarmed about Rowland's African interests. This he outlined in a highly confidential submission to the Monopolies Commission:

Lonrho is not just engaged in business in Africa: it is engaged heavily in politics. Rowland has intervened in several African crises, notably Sudan and Zimbabwe, and is actively concerned with the political future of many other states. There are several recent allegations about Lonrho's involvement in East African politics which are the subject of ongoing journalistic inquiry, some of them by the *Observer*.

And later, in a section called 'Rowland's Character', Trelford, after observing that Rowland did not have a scrupulous regard for the truth and the law, wrote:

. . . any pledges of editorial freedom and independence by Rowland have to be considered against this background. He is a man of powerful personality and immense resource – some would say ruthless in the pursuit of the company's interests . . . For Rowland to grant the *Observer* editorial independence would be to give one of his companies carte blanche to damage the whole business to which he has devoted his life.

The Monopolies Commission found in favour of Rowland's ownership and Trelford went on the attack again, slighting both the Commission and Rowland in public. It is a testament to Trelford's extraordinary skill as a politician that three years after he wrote the submission, he is still (at least at the time of writing) the editor of the *Observer*.

In fact he gives every appearance of working rather well under Tiny, even though, as he himself predicted, Mr Rowland has taken a close interest in the paper's African coverage; so close that in 1983 Tiny rang Trelford with the news that he had employed Godwin Matatu, on Lonrho's payroll, as the *Observer*'s resident correspondent in Zimbabwe. Trelford accepted Matatu without batting an eyelid, and had it not been for the *Observer*'s watchful staff the appointment would have gone unremarked. The union chapel decided to take it up with Rowland and after a long dispute Rowland eventually agreed to put Matatu on the *Observer* staff, which is probably what he wanted to do in the first place.

Trelford's submission to the Monopolies Commission was, it turned out, remarkably prescient, as his public dispute with Rowland over the events in Matabeleland proved. Here was the classic conflict of interest that he had predicted. The twenty-four hours he spent in Zimbabwe investigating the story of tribal massacres were perhaps inadequate, but he was well within his rights to publish. Indeed, subsequent revelations have largely borne him out. Rowland, having arranged Trelford's introductions to leading Zimbabwean politicians, expected an entirely different story and was outraged.

Trelford, with his usual nimble-footedness, made the row into an issue of press freedom, as indeed it was, and he stuck rigidly to his guns throughout the following ten days, during which he was subjected by Rowland to public abuse, financial intimidation, even threats that the paper would be sold. Suddenly it was all over, and after a flirtation with Robert Maxwell intended to put the wind up Trelford, the two men made their peace. Trelford had survived again.

THE TELEGRAPH GROUP
Daily Telegraph, Sunday Telegraph

LORD HARTWELL: PROPRIETOR

Lord Hartwell, the proprietor and editor-in-chief of the *Daily Telegraph* and *Sunday Telegraph*, is the last of the old-fashioned press barons. He inherited the *Daily Telegraph* from his father Lord Camrose at the age of forty-three, having edited the *Sunday Mail* in Glasgow and performed as an efficient Managing Editor at the *Financial Times*. Now in his early seventies, Hartwell, still upright, elegant and fit, shows no particular inclination to make way for either of his sons, Nicholas and Adrian. He still regularly works a six-day week in his comfortable private suite on the fifth floor of Peterborough Court, presiding over a remarkably successful operation. Unlike the other Fleet Street groups, the *Telegraph* has no outside assets to support it; Hartwell has steered the papers through the disputes and disruptions of the last two decades ever mindful of this fact. He is perhaps, the most knowledgable of proprietors in Fleet Street. He rarely speaks at the Newspaper Publishers' Association, but when he does his fellow proprietors listen carefully.

The *Telegraph* is a family business, and Hartwell runs the concern rather in the manner of the paternalist spirit of a small engineering firm in the Midlands between the wars. He has an unfailing faith in his product and a very clear idea of what his reader wants. Of late the paper has lost circulation but it still stands at one and a quarter million, far more than *The Times* and the *Guardian* together. His readership tends to be conservative, middle-class and middlebrow. Hartwell sees no reason to offend conventional tastes by undue change, which is why the paper's layout and tone is archaic. The paper is by far and away the most informative of the national dailies because of Hartwell's own distaste for ideas, the news content is extensive and on the whole less biased than other conservative papers.

There is, perhaps, one great drawback to the idea of the happy family enterprise. Hartwell is stricken with a crippling shyness, which limits his capacity to communicate with his employees. In a recent and surprisingly frank profile by Peregrine Worsthorne, Assistant Editor of the *Sunday Telegraph*, the daily discomfort of Hartwell arriving at work was thus recorded:

> As the car edges into Peterborough Court, the commissionaires, following a ritual established by his father, all leap to attention, rushing to hold lifts for the great man, brushing aside lesser mortals in paroxysms of deference that visibly cause their reluctant recipient agonies of embarrassment.

It is a standing joke among his staff that if he is caught in a lift with someone he will always ask, whatever their station, about the quality of the *Daily Telegraph* canteen. It is a stock question designed to carry him to the fifth floor without the need for a more taxing exchange. Everything about Hartwell seems to defy intimacy from his fellow man. As Worsthorne notes, he is rarely tempted into argument with his journalists, communicating his views by a series of frowns and barely articulated monosyllables. And, as if fearing some subconscious revelation, his handwriting is almost illegible and requires teams of *Telegraph* executives to decipher it.

On the two occasions that I have talked to Hartwell, it has been to discuss his entries in the Houses of Parliament Art Exhibition, which it must be said are as baffling in their subject matter as they are awkward in execution. He was never properly able to explain why he had committed a nude portrait of his grandson to canvas, or for that matter the scowling features of Winston Churchill's gardener. Somewhere in the Hartwell make-up there is a need for self-expression, but it seems that he has never acquired the means of overcoming his shyness, an extraordinary disability for a man in the communications business.

However, it would be misguided to view Hartwell as a one-dimensional oddity, sitting with his garden and ancient butler on top of the *Telegraph*. In the defence of the things that he cherishes he can be surprisingly fierce and effective. When Lord Lambton attacked Hartwell's late wife, Pamela, in a vitriolic profile published by Sir James Goldsmith in *Now!* magazine, he wrote a coruscating letter to Goldsmith describing Lambton as 'the man who idles on his vast estates and amuses himself by occasional spiteful attacks on his erstwhile friends. The man whose only excuse when surprised by *News of the World* photographers was "people sometimes like variety".' It is interesting that at the time of Lambton's fall Hartwell had disapproved of the *News of the World*'s activities, but when his wife was attacked he was happy to use them in her defence. He can be equally tough about his newspaper. When the *Sunday Telegraph* was censured by Jeremy Thorpe's counsel for buying the memoirs of the chief prosecution witness, Peter Bessell, Hartwell steeled himself to address the House of Lords and denounce the alliance of trial judge and counsel in discrediting the prosecution witnesses.

Hartwell's politics are undeclared but implicitly anti-socialist. The views of his papers are, of course, strongly in favour of the Conservative party, but this is not to say that coverage of the Labour party is any more biased than that of the *Daily Mail* or *The Times*. He strongly resists attempts by leading figures in either of the main parties to influence or criticise the content of his papers. And it is important to realise that this, the most privileged, traditional and conservative of press barons was made a life peer by Harold Wilson in 1968.

Hartwell's most fervent desire is that the two papers continue under the control of the Berry family, though it is still unclear whether Adrian or Nicholas, neither of whom seems wholly suitable, will inherit the paper. Nicholas, having worked on the *Telegraph*'s City pages, has left for the City itself, while Adrian remains on the paper as the Science Editor and regularly entertains readers with large spreads headlined DINOSAURS HAD DRY FEET IN WILTSHIRE or his musings on the nature of black holes or sub-atomic particles.

WILLIAM DEEDES: EDITOR, *Daily Telegraph*

William Deedes was chosen to edit the *Daily Telegraph* by Lord Hartwell in 1975 from a number of promising contenders which included Kenneth Fleet, Colin Welch and Andrew Alexander of the *Daily Mail*, all of whom are further to the right than Deedes. He was, at sixty-one, said to be fulfilling the role of caretaker while Hartwell made up his mind who would take the paper into the eighties. But caretakers have a habit of becoming tenants, and ten years later Bill Deedes's benign, elastic features are still occupying the editor's office.

It is the most engaging part of Deedes's biography that as a young man he was the main inspiration for William Boot, the nature-notes writer for the *Daily Beast* in Evelyn Waugh's novel *Scoop* who was mistakenly uprooted from monitoring the current affairs of the hedgerow and made a war correspondent. Deedes, in fact, shared a house with Waugh in Ethiopia and equipped himself with everything but Boot's cleft sticks to cover the Italian occupation. Unlike Boot he progressed in journalism to become a lobby correspondent and diplomatic reporter for the *Daily Telegraph*, during which time he travelled to Munich with Chamberlain. He entered the House of Commons in 1947 as the Conservative member for Ashford in Kent, an area which had been represented by his grandfather and great-grandfather and where his family had farmed since the last years of Henry VIII's reign. During his years on the back benches Deedes maintained his relationship with the *Telegraph* as the political correspondent for the paper's inoffensive gossip column, Peterborough. His time in the Macmillan cabinet does not seem to have been particularly successful. As a journalist he was given the job of overseeing the government's press relations, an uncomfortable position when the Profumo affair absorbed every journalist in Fleet Street. Deedes was naturally on the side of the press and did not perform especially well as a suppressor of information. He said, shortly afterwards, 'Newspapers do not exist to please politicians. They should be apart and even mistrustful of each other.' This now seems an odd remark when you consider the number of Conservative M.P.s spawned by Deedes's *Telegraph* and also the speechifying semi-intellectuals who are loaned out from Peterborough Court when the Conservative party feels the need to express itself.

Deedes's editorship has developed in a most original way. Soon after his appointment it was clear that Hartwell had no intention of letting him edit the whole paper and limited his jurisdiction to the leader page and the arts pages. The bulk of the paper is presided over by Peter Eastwood, a man of deep prejudices and irascible manner. This duumvirate neatly demonstrates Hartwell's distinction between the functions of his newspaper and, in the extent of Eastwood's control, emphasises his own preference for news rather than views. The relationship seems to work well enough, though this is more due to Deedes's equanimity than Eastwood's willingness to compromise. This distribution of power suits Hartwell perfectly. As Editor-in-Chief of the newspaper he does not expect opposition from his editor, and in real terms Deedes and Eastwood are his deputies. The latter has more power, but Deedes has more prestige.

Deedes serves as a remarkably effective ambassador for his paper. He still has close ties within the Conservative party and has never fallen into the trap of allying himself either to the Thatcherite or the wet camp of the party. Deedes is universally popular in the media and politics, engagingly lampooned in *Private Eye* and prized by politicians for his discretion.

Deedes is now seventy-two, and Hartwell must be thinking of ending his caretakership before he himself retires.

JOHN THOMPSON: EDITOR, *Sunday Telegraph*

By contrast to Lord Hartwell and William Deedes, John Thompson, the editor of the *Sunday Telegraph* is at sixty-four a mere stripling. What he lacks in years, though, he makes up with a slow seriousness and elderly caution. He was appointed to the important post of editor of the *Sunday Telegraph*, Hartwell's creation and prized possession, after a sound but not particularly glamorous career as a political writer for the *Evening Standard* and the *Spectator*, where he was also deputy editor. At the time of his surprising elevation from assistant editorship of the *Sunday Telegraph* one colleague said, 'John Thompson, though a nice man, rather nice, is a grey man – grey hair, grey eyes, grey suits and grey views, white shirt and black shoes.' He was, therefore, the perfect choice for the *Sunday Telegraph*, never the most daring or original of newspapers. Like Thompson it is prematurely aged and is characterised by an attitude which approaches all that is new with the deepest suspicion.

Thompson made his reputation as a writer in the sixties and was well known for the deftness of his political commentary in the *Evening Standard*. It is an odd fact that, while Deedes was the inspiration for William Boot, Thompson actually took up Boot's trade while working for the *Spectator*. Drawing on his experience of natural phenomena round his home at Much Hadham in Hertfordshire he compiled a column called 'Country Notebook', which was signed 'Peter Quince'. His observations were admired and were eventually published as a collection.

Despite his donnish appearance Thompson had a relatively humble background and did not go to university, which, one suspects, is the reason why he has such an intense admiration for academics who frequently appear in the columns of his newspaper. It may also go some way to explaining his preference for the sort of writing to be found in periodicals like the *Spectator*, which has lately supplied a number of contributors to the paper, including Alexander Chancellor, Auberon Waugh and Geoffrey Wheatcroft.

Thompson's most obvious characteristic is that he is retiring to the point of joining a trappist order. He does not like journalists who brag or who are over-endowed with self-confidence. In this he is clearly at one with his proprietor, and it is easy to see why Hartwell preferred him to Peregrine Worsthorne. Thompson was unlikely to go on television and bring the *Sunday Telegraph* into disrepute by using the word 'fuck' as Worsthorne had done. He is also, one suspects, a lot more malleable than Worsthorne and is more easily nagged into changing leader comments.

It is difficult to work up much feeling about Thompson; to say whether he is a good or bad editor or even a good or bad individual. His friends say that privately he is a generous and funny man but his public persona is balanced, rather dull and nondescript; adjectives which may easily be applied to his paper.

Stop Press: Robert Maxwell
and the Mirror Group

Much happened in the few weeks between the writing and proofreading of this book to strengthen some of the arguments in the preceding chapters. The Audit Bureau of Circulations (ABC), keenly watched by newspaper managements and the advertising industry, released figures for sales of national newspapers between January and June 1984. The most obvious and gratifying conclusion to draw from them is that Bingo has only a temporary effect on circulation. After the intense bingo war between the *Daily Express* and the *Daily Mail* in the autumn of 1983, sales of both newspapers have slipped, with the latter actually suffering a very slight loss. Mr Murdoch's papers continue to burgeon; the *News of the World* put on a little over 200,000, *The Times* went up by 45,000, the *Sunday Times* 25,000 and the *Sun* 16,000. There was little encouragement for Lord Hartwell in his group's figures; both the *Daily Telegraph* and *Sunday Telegraph* lost readers. The *Daily Express*, under the editorship of Sir Larry Lamb, recorded an overall increase of about 100,000, while its sister paper the *Sunday Express* was down 14,000. With the exception of the *Sunday Times*, all the up-market Sunday papers have been hit by the incredible growth of the *Mail on Sunday*, which looks more confident with every issue, and has gained some 270,000 readers in the last year. The Mirror Group, now under the ownership of Robert Maxwell, appears to have been affected by the constant uncertainty over its possible flotation; the *Daily Mirror* showed signs of catching the *Sun* by putting on 50,000 and the *Sunday Mirror* put on some 11,000; however, the *Sunday People* lost 15,000.

Here are the figures in full:

Title	Jan–June 1984	Jan–June 1983
Sun	4,186,907	4,170,909
Daily Mirror	3,365,293	3,315,070
Daily Star	1,370,942	1,337,486
Daily Express	1,981,675	1,891,270
Daily Mail	1,800,783	1,806,022
Daily Telegraph	1,259,519	1,266,069
Guardian	473,159	437,222
Times	381,075	336,189
Financial Times	216,440	215,570
News of the World	4,280,713	4,074,424
Sunday Mirror	3,523,000	3,512,228
Sunday People	3,377,282	3,392,746
Sunday Express	2,602,933	2,616,825
Mail on Sunday	1,584,707	1,307,060
Sunday Times	1,313,377	1,288,488
Observer	773,883	783,068
Sunday Telegraph	737,265	738,193

It is also worth mentioning two libel actions against national newspapers which have been heard in the High Court and are therefore freed from the sub-judice restrictions. Both serve to underline the argument that a good many exclusives in the press are either entirely manufactured or are culled from other sources. The first, predictably, involved the *Sun*, and was ostensibly an interview between the paper's Ian Todd and the former England test cricketer Graham Gooch. He was quoted as saying that he 'couldn't care less about England', which meant of course that he preferred to make a fat salary out of the game rather than play for his country. Todd's article would have been safe if Gooch had actually made the remark. The High Court ruled that the interview had never taken place and that the quotes in Mr Todd's Exclusive were the result of some lively speculation in the offices of the newspaper as to what the player might have been thinking. He was awarded £25,000 damages. In the same week the *Daily Mail* was ordered to pay substantial damages to Princess Yasmin Khan, the daughter of the late Aly Khan and the actress Rita Hayworth. Theirs was a ploy which is frequently used in Fleet Street, but which often goes unchallenged. The paper had published a series of articles about Princess Yasmin's mother under the general heading SECRETS OF A LOVE GODDESS. They were presented as the result of an exclusive interview with the Princess. This, of course, was not the case at all. The content had been in part lifted from an interview which the Princess had given in an American magazine in order to publicise the effects of Alzheimer's Disease, from which her mother now suffers. The rest was supplied by scurrilous biography which the *Daily Mail* cunningly wove into the original interview. The High Court decided that the *Daily Mail* had been dishonest in its presentation and ordered it to apologise, to pay costs and to make a substantial donation to the Alzheimer's Disease charity.

By far the most important recent event in Fleet Street is the arrival of Robert Maxwell at the Mirror Group. For well over a decade it has seemed inevitable that Maxwell, politician, publisher, patron of the arts, war hero and backer of Britain would acquire for himself that ultimate symbol of power and influence, a national newspaper. Since he was first beaten to the *News of the World* by the young Rupert Murdoch in 1969, Maxwell has pursued this goal more keenly than anything else in his business career. At every crisis or rumour of sale in Fleet Street Maxwell waited in the wings, but never managed to be more than understudy to Matthews, Murdoch and Tiny Rowland. In the last year his pursuit of a press baronetcy became even more urgent. He offered for the *Observer* during Rowland's public dispute with the editor, Donald Trelford. He unnerved Lord Matthews by a rapid acquisition of shares in Express Newspapers. And finally he began to make overtures to Reed International, the owners of the Mirror Group. At first his wooing of Sir Alex Jarratt seemed as forlorn as any of his other overtures to Fleet Street. The company had publicly stated its intention of floating the papers on the stock market, thus protecting them from the whim of a Murdoch or a Rowland. Clive Thornton, apparently a tough-minded and adventurous manager, had been made chairman to oversee the sale and to make the group into an attractive proposition. He had many good ideas, but embarrassed Reed's board of directors by making them public. There was a general feeling that he underestimated the difficulties of running a newspaper. At the beginning of July Maxwell made a verbal offer to Sir Alex in the knowledge that he would have to conclude a purchase before the flotation since Reed had secretly stipulated that no one individual would be allowed more than 15 per cent of the group. (Maxwell apparently had a source inside the group.) His first offer was pitched at £80 million, some £30 million above Reed's estimate of the group's minimum value on the stock-market. While the board agonised and prevaricated Maxwell swiftly announced that he would pay an extra £20 million. Finally, in the early hours of Friday July 13, Maxwell and Reed agreed a price of £113.4 million; like old masters newspapers are worth whatever people are prepared to pay for them, and Maxwell was as determined a bidder as Reed was ever likely to find.

He had moved deftly and with assurance. The success of his British Printing and Communications Corporation meant that he had almost unlimited finance available; he had, as it were, squared the government; and through his acquaintance Roy Hattersley he had ensured that there would be little opposition from the Labour party, although Neil Kinnock voiced some reservations.

The day after the announcement Maxwell took over the front page of the *Daily Mirror* to address his readers under the headline FORWARD WITH BRITAIN (The *New Statesman* suggested that, in view of the fact that Maxwell's holding company is registered in Vaduz, FORWARD WITH LIECHTENSTEIN might be more appropriate.) He promised that he would make the papers more efficient and profitable, that he would support the 'sensible left' and that he would fight complacency in every sector of British life. The persistent theme of the piece was its fervent patriotism. The phrase 'Forward with Britain' appears three times on that front page, odd when you consider Maxwell was born into an orthodox Jewish family in Podkarpaska Rus – Sub-Carpathian Russia, in what is now Czechoslovakia – in 1923.

He was named Jan Lodvic Hoch, although his family and friends appear to have called him Lajbi. There were seven children in the family, and his father, a farm labourer who occasionally worked as butcher, seems to have earned barely enough to keep them. Maxwell received little in the way of formal education, but he was prodigiously intelligent, adventurous and independent. As a teenager before the war he wandered between Poland, Hungary and Czechoslovakia, loosely attaching himself to various underground movements and anti-Nazi groups. Before his eighteenth birthday he was picked up by the security police in Budapest and sentenced to death by firing squad for his help in organising the escape of Czech dissidents. The sentence was commuted to imprisonment because of his youth, although he escaped jail with remarkable ease.

By 1940 Hoch had made his way to join the Légion Tchèque, which was fighting in southern France. He was described then as an 'unruly, unsophisticated boy from the mountains'. However, he showed an intense desire to improve himself, which he did among the educated members of this extraordinary military unit. By any standards Hoch, who variously adopted the names of du Maurier (after the brand of cigarettes) Jones and Maxwell, had a good war. A natural, if somewhat unorthodox leader, he was commissioned in the field for gallantry and in the closing weeks of the allied invasion of Germany was awarded the M.C. for an attack on a machine-gun position.

This, then, was Maxwell's youth. By the age of twenty-three he had acquired an opportunism, adaptability and independence which have served him well since. He had no ties with his homeland (his father had been shot by the Germans and his mother died in Auschwitz) and instead developed a profound admiration for the British.

The advantage of being an outsider in British society and business, particularly newspaper and book publishing, cannot, it seems, be overestimated. Like Rowland, Maxwell arrived in Britain unfettered by conventional notions of what was and what was not possible. Within a year of the end of hostilities Maxwell had bought his first holding, in a trading company named Low-Bell Ltd which thrived in a Europe starved of nearly every commodity. He used his connections with the occupying forces, in which, incidentally he had briefly served as a press censor, to buy the rights in valuable scientific material which had not been published in the allied countries for at least seven years. He also entered the wholesale book trade, taking over the ailing firm of Simpkin Marshall which, despite a promising start, was wound up by the Official Receiver in 1951. Maxwell claims to have lost £250,000, but others involved in the collapse believe that it was a great deal less. 'I've come down flat on my arse,' he said at the time, 'but I'm going up again and this time I'm staying up.'

He was not quite right in this forecast, which did as much as anything to earn him the nickname of 'Bouncing Czech'. At the end of the 1960s, when Maxwell proposed the merger of his Pergamon Press, which he had founded in 1951, with Saul Steinberg's Leasco, a city investigation revealed that he had been hugely optimistic about the profitability of Pergamon. There were a number of unorthodox devices in the company's accounts and a subsequent investigation by the Department of Trade declared in 1971 that 'Mr Maxwell is not in our opinion a person who can be relied upon to execute the proper stewardship of a publicly quoted company'.

This remark has dogged Maxwell for the past thirteen years. It was made a year after he lost his parliamentary seat (he had been Labour M.P. for Buckingham since 1964), and one would have thought that the combined failure of his political and business ambitions would have dealt him a considerable blow. Maxwell seems not to have cared very much. He said to the *Guardian*'s Terry Coleman, 'Now, you have met a man who doesn't care a fig about the loss of a seat. If I am wanted to be of service, I'll give my best. But the minute I am not wanted I'll leave as if I have never been there.' In truth his parliamentary career had not been spectacularly successful. He served on various Commons committees but was never awarded the high office to which he undoubtedly felt himself suited. He never got over the Labour party's instinctive dislike of socialist millionaires and was treated with the utmost suspicion by many of his fellow backbenchers.

Nevertheless Maxwell, one of the richest men in the country, still cherishes the socialist tradition. He recently financed the Labour Party's case against the changes made by the Boundaries Commission, and gives generously to the party.

A couple of years after the Department of Trade enquiry, Maxwell regained control of Pergamon and began to build an extraordinarily successful publishing business, specialising in the scientific and educational fields. It became the vehicle for the takeover of the British Printing Corporation (he changed the title to British Printing and Communications Corporation), and he set about planning B.P.C.C.'s revitalisation by concentrating on the company's more efficient plants and by taking on the printing unions.

In his own words he looks as if he is staying up for good. However, this was little consolation for panic-stricken Mirror Group journalists, who were appalled that Reed's principles could so easily be bought by the man they considered the least desirable proprietor around. Nor were they encouraged by Maxwell's only previous foray into daily newspaper ownership at the *Scottish Daily News*. While Maxwell is no doubt perfectly capable of managing the Mirror Group and making a profit, he is, as a *Sunday Times* profile put it, a 'fundamentally unpredictable and authoritarian personality armed with the powerful weapons of rationalism'. Others who have encountered his unpredictability and authoritarianism at first hand might put it more directly: he is generally held to be impossible to work for. Despite his avowed socialism and adherence to democratic systems he has little patience with opposition or argument from his employees. He made this clear when negotiating with Tiny Rowland for the *Observer*. Asked about his view of the paper's campaign for enlightenment on Mark Thatcher's business activities in Oman, Maxwell replied: 'If I had a battle with Trelford it would have been over Mark Thatcher. I would have sacked him absolutely. And despite what the independent directors or the government or anyone else wants to say, I would have sacked him on the spot.'

Leaving aside the question of whether and when it is right to float an unsubstantiated story in the public interest, Maxwell's attitude does not bode well for intransigent editors or journalists. The initial fuss, fuelled in part by Clive Thornton's very public outrage, has died down somewhat, though opinion is still sharply divided as to whether Maxwell's advent is a good thing or not. Maxwell and his editors have swapped expressions of mutual regard. Support has come from some unlikely sources: Joe Haines's outright opposition disappeared more or less overnight; Paul Johnson, writing in the *Spectator*, welcomed him on the grounds that he could neutralise dangerous lefties such as Paul Foot and John Pilger. (Johnson's piece, though not the journalists' stinging replies, was reprinted in *Mirror Group News* on Maxwell's instructions.) Certainly Maxwell's odd blend of cheap patriotism and middle-of-the-road socialism makes it difficult to assess the direction he will take. He has made various assurances, notably that he will not interfere with the editorial content of the papers (FORWARD WITH BRITAIN notwith-standing), and that he will take the *Daily Mirror* up-market, making it a more campaigning paper and leaving the *Sun* and the *Star* floundering in a morass of bingo and nudes. Such assurances are, of course, standard practice for incoming newspaper proprietors, and Mirror Group journalists would be wise not to place too much faith in them. In the meantime they, like everybody else, can only wait and see.

Index